GRANTMAKING
Basics

A Field Guide for Funders

By Barbara D. Kibbe, Fred Setterberg and Colburn S. Wilbur

With Jan Masaoka on "Numbers and Sense: Learning to Look at Nonprofit Finances"

VISION

The Council's vision for the field is of

A vibrant, growing and responsible philanthropic sector that advances the common good.

We see ourselves as part of a broad philanthropic community that will contribute to this vision. We aim to be an important leader in reaching the vision.

MISSION

The Council on Foundations provides the opportunity, leadership and tools needed by philanthropic organizations to expand, enhance and sustain their ability to advance the common good.

To carry out this mission, we will be a membership organization with effective and diverse leadership that helps the field be larger, more effective, more responsible and more cooperative.

By *common good* we mean the sum total of conditions that enable community members to thrive. These achievements have a shared nature that goes beyond individual benefits.

By *philanthropic organizations* we mean any vehicle that brings people together to enhance the effectiveness, impact and leverage of their philanthropy. This includes private and community foundations, corporate foundations and giving programs, operating foundations, and public foundations, as well as emerging giving and grantmaking mechanisms involving collective participation.

STATEMENT OF INCLUSIVENESS

The Council on Foundations was formed to promote responsible and effective philanthropy. The mission requires a commitment to inclusiveness as a fundamental operating principle and calls for an active and ongoing process that affirms human diversity in its many forms, encompassing but not limited to ethnicity, race, gender, sexual orientation, economic circumstance, disability and philosophy. We seek diversity in order to ensure that a range of perspectives, opinions and experiences are recognized and acted upon in achieving the Council's mission. The Council also asks members to make a similar commitment to inclusiveness in order to better enhance their abilities to contribute to the common good of our changing society.

© 2005 Council on Foundations, Inc. All rights reserved.

© 1999, The David and Lucile Packard Foundation and the Council on Foundations, Inc. All rights reserved.

Library of Congress Cataloging-in-Publication Data

Kibbe, Barbara.

  Grantmaking basics : a field guide for funders / by Barbara D. Kibbe, Fred Setterberg, and Colburn S. Wilbur.
     p. cm.

  "With Jan Masaoka on "Numbers and Sense: Learning to Look at Nonprofit Finances."

  Includes index.

  ISBN 0-913892-75-0

  1. Nonprofit organizations–Management. 2. Nonprofit organizations–Evaluation. 3. Evaluation research (Social action programs) 4. Corporate governance. I. Setterberg, Fred. II. Wilbur, Colburn S. III. Title.

  HD62.6.K52 2005

  658.15'3—dc22

                        2005028898

THE DAVID AND LUCILE PACKARD FOUNDATION

300 2nd Street, Suite 200
Los Altos, CA 94022
650/948-7658
www.packfound.org

1828 L Street, NW, Suite 300
Washington, DC 20036-568
202/466-6512 ■ 202/785-3926
www.cof.org

As the central function of foundations, grantmaking is based on the assumptions that judicious funding decisions are possible and that foundations strive to make purposeful, not arbitrary, choices. Grantmaking is not the simplistic measuring of applications by rigid rules or standards, but a complex cultural understanding governed by powerful individual and organizational values. Grantmaking is an art, not a science, and its dimensions are not only intellectual, but aesthetic and moral as well.

How Foundations Work: What Grantseekers Need to Know about the Many Faces of Foundations
Dennis P. McIlnay
Jossey-Bass Publishers, 1998

Table of Contents

Foreword vii

Acknowledgments ix

About the Authors xi

Preface xiii

Introduction xv

CHAPTER 1 Welcome to the Working Week: Roles, Responsibilities, Obstacles and Opportunities in a Grantmaker's Life 1

CHAPTER 2 Panning for Gold: How to Review Grant Proposals 15

CHAPTER 3 Conducting Site Visits and Interviews: A Guide for Program Officers 27

CHAPTER 4 Numbers and Sense: Learning to Look at Nonprofit Finances 45

CHAPTER 5 Between You and Your Board: Decisions, Recommendations and the Art of Communication 67

CHAPTER 6 Getting Better All the Time: Cultivating Professional Skills throughout Your Career 75

Appendix to Chapter 1 81

Appendix to Chapter 2 85

Appendix to Chapter 3 87

Appendix to Chapter 5 95

Appendix to Chapter 6 101

Glossary 103

Index 117

Foreword

This book is the result of several careers' worth of knowledge about the field of grantmaking. As the old saying goes: Learn from the wisdom of others because there isn't enough time to make all the mistakes yourself.

This book is written for all grantmakers, regardless of whether you come from a community, independent, public, family, non-U.S. or corporate foundation or corporate giving program. I hope you will find it helpful as you journey your way through your career.

Grantmaking Basics: A Field Guide for Funders is a joint publication of the Council on Foundations and the David and Lucile Packard Foundation. It is also the first in a series of grantmaking basics books on topics such as monitoring and evaluation, convening, grantmaking styles and strategies, boards and board-staff relationships, and capacity-building and technical assistance.

Grantmaking Basics: A Field Guide for Funders was made possible by a generous financial contribution by the David and Lucile Packard Foundation. Special thanks to authors Barbara D. Kibbe, Fred Setterberg, Colburn S. Wilbur and Jan Masaoka for putting down on paper their expertise. The field will benefit from their wisdom.

Dorothy S. Ridings
President and CEO
September 1999

Acknowledgments

Grantmaking Basics: A Field Guide for Funders is born of close collaboration, informed by the vision of many people within the funding world. We owe a special debt to Thomas C. Layton and Paul Ylvisaker, who inspired us and who remain role models for us in our own grantmaking.

In preparing the manuscript, we relied on numerous interviews with senior grantmakers throughout the country and submitted successive drafts of the manuscript to a peer review panel established through the Council on Foundations. In so doing, we benefited by an incalculable degree from the experience of our colleagues who generously shared their insights. We offer a special thanks to these essential advisors: Brock Adler, Doug Bauer, Dave Bergholz, Harriet Glickman, Sunshine Janda Overkamp, Lisa Parker, Cindy Raab, Molly Stearns, as well as to Bruce Sievers and Tom David.

We also want to offer our heartfelt and sincere thanks to those who tirelessly assisted us in preparing, producing and publishing *Grantmaking Basics*, especially Pamela Lawrence, but also Gwen Foster, Richard Green, Kimberly Hsieh, Phyllis Jask, Mark Jansen, Linda Laird, Wendy-Ellen Ledger and Leslie Welch.

Any misperceptions or idiosyncratic convictions remain, of course, our own responsibility.

About the Authors

Barbara D. Kibbe is director, Organizational Effectiveness Program, and director, Program Officer Training and Development, at the David and Lucile Packard Foundation. She brings nearly 20 years experience in nonprofit management and consulting to the foundation. She began her career with nonprofits as executive director of Bay Area Lawyers for the Arts in 1978. From 1987 through 1993, Kibbe was a partner in Harder & Kibbe Research & Consulting, a firm working exclusively with nonprofit organizations and public sector agencies.

Kibbe was interim director of the Bay Area Discovery Museum in Sausalito, California, supervising a 12-member management team and a staff of nearly 70. While at the museum, she provided leadership in facilitating the design, development and installation of a new permanent exhibition.

Kibbe is active as a mediator and arbitrator with the Arts Arbitration and Mediation Services Program of California Lawyers for the Arts, a program she helped to found while executive director of that agency.

Kibbe graduated *cum laude* and with departmental honors in art from Wagner College in New York City and earned a law degree from Brooklyn Law School.

Fred Setterberg is the co-author of two previous books about the nonprofit sector: *Succeeding with Consultants* written with Barbara Kibbe, published by the Foundation Center Press, and *Beyond Profit: The Complete Guide to Managing the Nonprofit Organization*, written with Kary Schulman, and published by Harper & Row.

His other books include *The Roads Taken: Travels through America's Literary Landscapes*, published by Interlink Books, winner of the Associated Writing Program's award in creative nonfiction; *Toxic Nation: The Fight to Save Our Communities from Chemical Contamination*, written with Lonny Shavelson, and published by John Wiley and Sons; and *Travelers' Tales America*, published by Travelers' Tales Guides, which he edited.

Setterberg is the recipient of a National Endowment for the Arts creative writing fellowship and numerous journalism awards.

Colburn S. Wilbur is a trustee and former president and CEO of the David and Lucile Packard Foundation. He led the foundation for 23 years. Prior to that, he served as executive director and CEO of the Sierra Club Foundation, worked in international banking as well as for a computer service bureau.

He currently serves on the boards of Philanthropic Ventures Foundation, the Sierra Club Foundation and the Stanford Theatre Foundation. His past board affiliations include the Council on Foundations, the Foundation Center, Big Brothers of San Francisco and the Peninsula, Northern California Grantmakers, Peninsula Grantmakers, the Global Fund for Women, the Peninsula Conservation Center, the Dominican College International Graduate Studies Program, and the University of San Francisco Institute for Nonprofit Management.

Wilbur received both his undergraduate and MBA degrees from Stanford University.

Jan Masaoka is executive director of the Support Center for Nonprofit Management, one of the country's leading providers of technical assistance to nonprofit organizations. As staff consultant, Masaoka consults to nonprofit organizations on financial management, executive director succession and boards of directors.

Masaoka authored *All Hands on Board* (published by the National Center for Nonprofit Boards), *Finance Manual for Nonprofits* (published by the National Minority AIDS Council) and she edits the *Board Café*, a national newsletter for nonprofit board members, which has more than 7,000 subscribers.

In addition to conference keynotes, Masaoka is a frequent seminar leader on the use of financial information in grantmaking. Masaoka's community activities include serving as president of the San Francisco Foundation Community Initiative Funds and vice president of the San Francisco Telecommunications Commission.

In August of 1999 she was named by *Nonprofit Times* as one of the "50 Most Influential People" in the nonprofit sector nationwide.

Preface

Grantmaking Basics: A Field Guide for Funders is both a guide and a workbook for those involved in the grantmaking process of a foundation or corporation. This book is arranged in an easy-to-read style—highlight it, refer to it often, tear out its pages—it is subsidized to make it less expensive. It is designed to be a book for one person to use and refer to often rather than read and put away. There are many good ideas that will hopefully stimulate the readers to perform better and enjoy their work.

Barbara Kibbe and Fred Setterberg have spent countless hours working on this book. They have years of experience and have spoken with many knowledgeable and thoughtful grantmakers in preparing the following information. I am very fortunate to have my name associated with their dedicated and excellent efforts.

Using this book should greatly enhance one's abilities. Many program staff work alone or with little assistance in the grant review process. The applicants will not complain to our face or provide us with a list of shortcomings and neither will our colleagues. This guide should provide even the most experienced with some new ideas.

In 1976, when I started at the David and Lucile Packard Foundation as the half-time CEO with a half-time assistant, the trustees assumed that I knew the subjects considered within this book. Fortunately because of some previous experience at the Sierra Club Foundation, I knew some, but I had not been adequately trained. Foundation staff are hired from a variety of backgrounds and we somehow expect them to be capable, from the start, of reviewing proposals, understanding financial reports, making site visits and interviewing applicants.

It is a strange situation in which we find ourselves: so much responsibility coupled with so little preparation. No other industry would consider hiring inexperienced employees without rigorous training and well-crafted plans for professional development. But program staff have always occupied an odd position in philanthropy. I can think of no other sector in American society that fails to provide its key employees with the training they need to reap the intended results. In the foundation world—despite the billions of dollars we oversee and the pressing problems we confront—we have had to fight our way through the thicket pretty much on our own.

I am happy to say that this situation is beginning to change. A handful of foundations have now developed programs for training their own program officers. In recent years, the Council on Foundations and several regional associations of grantmakers have also emerged as useful resources. Even the literature is growing—both the academic analyses of foundation giving patterns and the occasional tract on sound practice. In short, we know a good deal more about what it takes to be an effective program officer than we did 25 years ago.

Unfortunately, most foundation professionals still do not have an opportunity to benefit from this knowledge. National and regional trainings are only infrequently offered. People laboring outside of large metropolitan areas seldom have a chance to confer and learn from their peers.

Grantmaking Basics: A Field Guide for Funders seeks to aid people who have not had the benefit of formal training. It includes humor, practical advice and philosophy. It speaks from the experience of many of us who have been working in this field during the past several decades and struggling to shape the standards of our profession. It is both a primer for people entering philanthropy and a set of reminders for veterans who might benefit from taking a second look at the way things have "always been done" at their foundations.

Of course, our book does not pretend to be the last word on the subject. Rather, it is something of an opening bid—an invitation for you to join in the crucial conversation now taking place about the goals, standards and best practices of our profession. It is a conversation that we hope will continue for many years to come. Indeed, our purposes will be served if this book can engage, stimulate, amuse, provoke and, finally, assist our peers in their daily tasks of helping to change the world.

This book is not the complete answer to well-trained program officers, but at least it helps. If, as you use it, you can think of additions or changes, please let me know. Another edition can be written.

Colburn S. Wilbur
Trustee, Former President and CEO
The David and Lucile Packard Foundation

Introduction

Waking Up in the Grantmaker's World
A Guide for the Passionate, the Perplexed and the Recently Arrived

If you are like the vast majority of individuals who wake up one day to find themselves to be grantmakers, you have probably recognized within yourself the deeper rumblings of curiosity, doubt and perhaps even apprehension. Without a question, you are entering new territory.

Exactly what will your duties entail? What are your roles and responsibilities? Where can you pick up the basics and chart the subtle byways of philanthropy? What constitutes success in this field—or something less? Will you measure up to the job?

Your friends may not prove very helpful. Like the rest of the world, most of your intimates will never have guessed that several thousand people rise from bed every morning to labor each day as grantmakers until you tell them about your new job. Former colleagues in the nonprofit sector may share their personal opinions regarding philanthropy's value and shortcomings—perceptions often honed to a sharpened edge through the pursuit of funding for their own organizations. But few outsiders have caught more than a glimpse of the world you now inhabit.

Grantmaking Basics: A Field Guide for Funders aims to serve as a tool for individuals substantially responsible for the decisions and operations of a charitable foundation or corporate giving program.

For most of this country's nearly 50,000 foundations, that means a single paid staff person (working with or without administrative support) or an active volunteer from the board. It is for the people working in these foundations as well as new program staff at larger foundations—passionate about their work but frequently overburdened and isolated—that this book was written.

Grantmaking Basics: A Field Guide for Funders should prove useful for:

- Foundation/corporate giving staff new to the job.
- Experienced professionals who may wish to reflect upon their experience in the field.
- Board members and other leaders of foundations and corporate grantmaking programs.
- Anybody who reviews grant requests, including staff in government agencies.
- Nonprofit professionals curious about the foundation world's interior complexities.

Open and Use

How might you use this book to best effect? Readers can move through the material by several different routes.

For the person new to the job of program officer, foundation board member or corporate giving officer, it might be best to read *Grantmaking Basics: A Field Guide for Funders* straight through to orient yourself to some of the guiding principles and work routines of a funder's life. More seasoned professionals might turn to the book as a reference, sorting through the index for specific information about conducting site visits, what to do when a proposal's budget and narrative reflect opposing realities or a host of other matters. Mark the book up, scrawl notes to yourself in the margins, feel free to creatively dismantle its pages. The tools and worksheets are designed to be torn out and taken with you as a companion in the field.

New Series for Foundation Professionals

Grantmaking Basics: A Field Guide for Funders is the first book in a projected series of six self-study guides intended to advance the skills of grantmaking professionals and volunteers. During the next several years, this volume will be joined by complementary books on grantmaking styles and strategies, monitoring and evaluation, convening, boards and board/staff relationships, capacity-building and technical assistance. As these books assemble on the shelf to constitute a small library of practical assistance, we hope they will provide guidance to grantmakers, provoke debate and discussion and whet the funding community's growing appetite for improving its own performance in the continuous struggle to help improve the world.

CHAPTER 1

Welcome to the Working Week

Roles, Responsibilities, Obstacles and Opportunities in a Grantmaker's Life

Good grantmakers grow slowly into their duties. That is less a comment about program officers than the peculiarities of the job. Foundation work is different from most professions. Some seasoned hands even argue that it is not a profession. It is more of a trade, a calling, an avocation, an occupational odd-step on the unpredictable career ladder of sharp-witted, enthusiastic people with a commitment to the common good.

No matter. Let us just assume for the moment that life in a foundation is not quite like anything else you have previously encountered in your career.

To begin, almost everybody in the foundation world today came from someplace else. Typically, foundations draw their staff from individuals more thoroughly versed in the other side of nonprofit endeavor. They come from community agencies, service providers, think tanks, universities and other institutions that directly apply themselves to the task of improving the world: the seekers, rather than the givers of grants. Corporate giving programs are typically staffed or overseen by managers from the public relations or marketing side of the company. And even though there are a growing number of graduate and certificate programs in nonprofit management (and a small number of courses in philanthropy), few foundation or corporate giving officers land in their jobs fresh out of school. Indeed, grantmaking is one of the rare important occupations in our society that until quite recently has been obscured from the public sightlines. When pressed to reminisce about their first days on the job, many of the field's most productive veterans speak about their initial astonishment at finding themselves in their new role.

Neither do professional grantmakers constitute a very large world. Despite the substantial number of new foundations established during the economic booms of the 1980s and 1990s, there simply are not many jobs available. Many of the nation's nearly 50,000 foundations remain unstaffed. Among staffed foundations, you are likely to find one or two people toiling away in a small office in relative obscurity.

© Council on Foundations, Inc.

Yet if the ranks of foundation professionals appear slim and slightly obscure, we should not minimize the influence and importance of our role.

Each year, foundations and corporate giving programs disburse billions of dollars. They support programs and projects meant to improve the lives of people throughout the world and protect the world itself with all its precious ecosystems.

The people in charge of deciding where this money will go, however, are not career politicians, lifelong civil servants or even trained philanthropists. For the most part, they are people like you: capable, responsible, passionate, eager, experienced in other endeavors. Almost nobody enters their job with formal training.

Fortunately, there is a strong and growing national network of regional associations of grantmakers (RAGs) and funder affinity groups that can link colleagues working in similar fields across the country and, increasingly, the world.[1] Yet for most people, the best place to learn about the job—or improve skills—is on the job.

What it Takes to Get the Work Done

SKILLS AND ATTRIBUTES OF A SUCCESSFUL GRANTMAKER

If the odd dimensions and culture of foundation philanthropy were not enough, there is one more aspect of grantmaking that further complicates your role. The problem: You are charged with ensuring public benefit through the wise and timely distribution of funds to productive and well-run nonprofit organizations. Unfortunately, results in the nonprofit sector are notoriously difficult to measure.

Unlike the business world, the nonprofit sector seldom offers a reliable bottom line to demonstrate whether investments of money, time, hope and energy have proven successful. It is difficult to assess the likelihood of a proposed project reaping its intended benefits and even harder to predict. Nevertheless, you may be expected to render this kind of judgement hundreds or even thousands of times throughout your career.

To make sense of the complex process of judging the potential of any proposal, project or organization, program officers must cultivate five essential skills.

1. Ability to recognize what your board wants to support.

All your work should be based on a clear understanding of your foundation's values and mission. Does your board want to fund efforts in health, education and welfare or does it prefer projects that support scientific research and the environment? Are board members inclined to nourish start-up projects with seed money or provide long-term support for established organizations? Is the emphasis on expanding knowledge, influencing policy or providing direct services? Is the bulk of your funding local, regional, national or international? What is the policy on general operating support, endowments, reserve funds, building campaigns?

---

[1] Please see the Appendix to Chapter 1 for contact information on RAGs, funder affinity groups and detailed information on the programs and services of the Council on Foundations.

The clearer your foundation's vision, the more specific your goals—and the keener your board members' ability to articulate their preferences—the easier your job will be. Wealth does not wipe away the dilemmas of choice. No matter how much money your foundation accumulates, the number of potential funding opportunities will always outstrip your financial resources. Without direction from your board, you will find it a bewildering experience to sort through these myriad opportunities.

2. Knowledge of the fields funded by your foundation.

Throughout your career, you may be asked to render judgements on the value of everything from arts to zoos. Forget about becoming an expert in each of these areas; nobody can. But over time, you should be able to cultivate a basic understanding of the fields funded by your foundation so that you can knowledgeably enter into the conversation, review most proposals, provide intelligent analysis and make appropriate decisions.

Indeed, as you work with a growing roster of nonprofit collaborators, your knowledge base will expand accordingly. You will sharpen your insights and deepen your understanding of the background issues. You will read the hundredth proposal that comes across your desk on land use management with far greater acuity and imagination than the first one you encounter. You will come to instinctively (and cognitively) separate the promising organization from the long-range liability, the healthy plan from the good intention.

Successful foundation officers tend to be smart, intuitive, hard-working and analytically inclined. They are also honest about their ignorance. Nobody expects you to know as much about the issues as the specialists working inside the organizations funded by your foundation. You are, however, expected to listen, learn and keep learning. Good foundation officers invite applicant organizations to advance the grantmaker's education without unduly adding to the group's burden in the process. They seek assistance from outside experts and leading practitioners. They read a great deal, think about what they have read and discuss it whenever possible with their colleagues. In short, they relish their continuing acquisition of knowledge. They are hungry to learn more. They exercise, nurture and prize their own curiosity.

3. Grasp of the context within your funding strategy.

Beyond separating promising projects and organizations from risky bets, you must also grasp how a proposed effort aligns with your overall grantmaking portfolio. You must ask yourself if a project fits with similar ones already being funded. Does it complement your foundation's long-range funding goals? Is it embarking on an innovative approach with real potential or relying on proven methodologies aligned with well-documented best practices? Will it unconsciously duplicate efforts or will it add to the programmatic and geographic mix? Does the project serve the demonstrated needs of the target populations you are committed to serving?

In some foundations and corporate giving programs, the board might discuss every grant, grappling with the question of context on a continuing basis. In others, the board will establish broad funding guidelines, relying on the staff's discretion to calculate each project's suitability. But in all cases the issue of context remains crucial. In fact, it is entirely possible for program officers to recognize the board's funding priorities, understand the field and still make poor funding decisions if they are not cognizant of the context.

Let us take an example. Imagine that for the past decade you have been funding public health programs in the San Francisco Bay Area. Now your board has decided to expand programming to Denver, Colorado. You correctly perceive your foundation's funding priorities and you have learned a great deal about public health. But do you know anything about Denver?

In this case, context becomes your first priority. You must learn about other public health organizations and projects operating in Denver. You need to identify local problems, leaders, resources and opportunities—uncovering both alliances and rivalries. You have to know the history and prior funding patterns of ongoing efforts. These key contextual questions will shape your ability to make a good grant recommendation.

4. Ability to synthesize large amounts of information and communicate its essence to the board.

During the course of your work, you will necessarily seek out and sort through masses of complex information, digest it and turn it into short, effective pieces of analytical writing that justify your grant recommendations. Your board will read these analyses and then accept or reject them.

This ability to grasp the big picture is linked to the other skills that we have already mentioned. It presumes that you have correctly calculated a project's fit with your foundation, understood the relevant field and recognized its contextual implications. It also presumes that you are able to handle the volume of proposals and manage your time effectively, especially if you are the only staff member.

5. Ability to communicate.

The clarity of your judgments and the quality of your recommendations hinge upon your ability to communicate. Good communication begins with good listening. Over time, you will need to extend your capacity for paying keen, patient attention to grantseekers, board members and experts in the field. Without strong listening skills, you own words will soon degenerate into pompous pronouncements. You will neglect crucial opportunities for leaning, and cling too tightly and too long to your own biases.

Beyond Skills

Aside from these five keystone skills, what else might we say about the successful foundation professional or volunteer?

In terms of personality, successful grantmakers tend to be optimistic. They believe that their efforts make a difference in the world; that is why they come to work each day. Over time, this innate optimism is reinforced by a clear-eyed view of their foundation's performance and their own part in advancing its mission.

That is not to say program officers should be entirely credulous. A dose of skepticism enables everybody to keep a healthy check on inflated expectations. (Now and then, you may help change the world in important ways, but you will never achieve its total reformation.) Simply giving away money is not the point. You want to see the proof of results.

Good program officers also exhibit drive. Rather than functioning as cogs in the machine, they emerge as the animating force that propels the foundation toward its goals. (Think of yourself immodestly as the spark plug, the engine and the steering wheel rolled into one.) Effectiveness in the foundation world demands self-confidence but not arrogance. Good grantmakers will occasionally urge, prod and push their board to question its own assumptions (and be willing to accept the fact that their own recommendations might not be taken). They volunteer to entertain a degree of personal discomfort for the greater good—the irritant in the oyster that forms the pearl. Over time, they will know when to look beyond the feasible practicalities of routine grantmaking to argue in favor of visionary possibilities.

A Growth Opportunity

Many program officers join the foundation world after years of direct service in education, child development, social welfare, the environment or other fields. They bring to grantmaking an enviable insider's familiarity with the programs they are now charged with reviewing for funding. As former service providers, they speak the same language as the applicants; they find it easy to establish trust. Their presence serves as a hedge against the apathy or arrogance that can arise when funders lack real-world experience in the nonprofit sector.

Yet to blossom fully as program officers, they may need to complement their practical experience with theoretical knowledge. They may have to acquaint themselves with their field's history, controversies and hidden opportunities. Perhaps they may need to cultivate their understanding of organizational theory and nonprofit management, including planning, budgeting and evaluation.

Other grantmakers are hired precisely because of their theoretical sophistication. They may be former policymakers, researchers or university professors. Their task will be to deepen their theoretical knowledge with on-site experience, visiting organizations in the field and learning directly from the frontline staff.

In other words, nobody ever comes to this job knowing everything they need. Program officers are always asked to stretch; flexibility is an entry-level requirement. Indeed, the opportunity to assume the role of life-long learner is one of job's most delectable benefits.

In most cases, professional development will originate from two sources.

Research. Some program officers will need to undertake a course of serious, self-directed study, acquainting themselves with the key theoretical and organizational texts related to their foundation's interest areas. They will conduct informational interviews with community leaders, academics and practitioners in various fields. New grantmakers should also strive to understand the history of philanthropy; in particular, they should study the course of grantmaking in their foundation's primary fields.

Relationships. Program officers will also profit from ongoing professional relationships with their peers. For most grantmakers who work in one-person offices, these relationships may take some initial effort to construct. They will need to seek out potential colleagues who may be working in other foundations or corporate giving programs, the United Way or government funding agencies. Foundation staff

Trends: More or Less

When asked to remark on recent trends in grantmaking, funders interviewed for the Foundation Center's *Guide to Proposal Writing* saw several. In shorthand, they are as follows:

- More competition for every dollar, partly due to less government money available.
- More emphasis on evaluation and "knowing how to recognize accomplishments."
- More requests and higher sophistication of requests.
- Grantmakers looking more closely for indicators of a nonprofit's stability—in leadership, in planning, in finances.
- More mergers and collaborations among grantees.
- More direct service and less policy/advocacy projects.
- Fewer multiyear grant awards.
- More capital campaign requests.
- More requests for funds for hiring development staff.
- More management assistance grants.
- More requests for computer assistance: hardware, software, training.

Geever, Jane C. "The Unwritten Rules About Proposals Written Down." *Foundation News & Commentary,* March/April 1997, pp. 30–34.

Jane C. Geever is a professional fundraiser. Original article excerpted with permission

located outside of large urban areas may need to exert extra effort in seeking out peers at conferences, through the Council on Foundations, among regional associations and affinity groups that they join or start on their own. Program officers might also cultivate professional relationships with scholars, independent researchers and journalists with whom they can maintain a continuing conversation about their communities' needs and assets.

Occupational Hazards

PROBLEMS THAT WILL TRIP YOU UP (IF YOU ARE NOT LOOKING)

Even the most rewarding occupations carry liabilities. In the foundation world, your own set of occupational hazards will not prove as serious as others. Nevertheless, they can prove irritating, confounding and potentially damaging if you do not anticipate their presence and then finesse your way through them.

Occupational Hazard 1: Wherever you go, the money will follow.

Once you become a program officer, it has been frequently quipped, you will never have a bad meal or a bad idea. People will accommodate you lavishly, even shamelessly. After all, they reason, you do appear to hold the purse strings. (Why not laugh at your jokes, echo your opinions, massage your vanity?) Even in the most open and honest relationships, the money will stick by your side—the silent partner in all conversations.

The money also serves as an unofficial bodyguard. Like it or not, you are now shielded from criticism's more pointed barbs, some of which might inspire (or otherwise motivate) improvements in your foundation's methods and your own job performance. People may gripe about not getting a grant, but they are unlikely to recite in penetrating detail your philanthropic failings. Too dangerous. That means the onus for improvement-through-self-criticism falls squarely, exclusively, on you. It can be a heavy burden.

You will also find out who your friends are. (Hint: They are probably not the people you once vaguely knew in another life who now seem so terribly interested in lunching and schmoozing.) Suddenly, everybody wants something from you; they want the money. This can prove a jarring, even hurtful experience. You may find yourself thinking twice before showing up in public. ("Will my presence at Saturday's concert elicit an unwanted grant proposal on my desk Monday morning?") You will endure a deluge of invitations for social events that are actually bids for business contacts.

Try not to take it personally. Recognize that the job, after all, is only the job. Concentrate on your family, your tried and trusted friends. Admit to yourself that your sudden overwhelming popularity owes much to the proximity of potential riches. Remind yourself that the enormous expectations of grantseekers are often linked to their vision of a better world—something you share. Strive to remain gracious in the face of their hope, fear and urgency. Resolve to lead as normal a professional life as possible.

Occupational Hazard 2: The power.

As a conduit to the money that now dogs your every step, you will also be accompanied by a sizeable dose of power. There is no way around this. For all the talk about "partnership" and "collaboration"—ideals toward which you should genuinely strive—you must finally admit that in every encounter with grantseekers, you hold most of the cards. There is nothing inherently wrong with this arrangement; it is life. The problems arise when you fail or refuse to acknowledge the disparity in power that separates you and the people seeking your support.

Some foundation people succumb to power poisoning. They indulge themselves in arrogant behavior that the rest of the world rightly perceives to be crude, insensitive and ridiculous. (We recently heard about a program officer who proudly proclaimed her habit of tossing out any proposal that had misspelled her name. If this is not the height of reckless arrogance, it is certainly reaching for the loftier peaks.) Beware of colleagues who brag about their intolerance, impatience and impossibly high standards.

Also keep in mind: It is not your money. Do not over-identify with your professional role. You are only watching over your foundation's wealth until somebody else can be found who will put it to best use.

There is also another kind of arrogance, less obvious and perhaps more insidious. It is the arrogance of dispensing gratuitous advice. The temptation can be great. Grantseekers will always listen politely and agree with you even when they suspect that you don't know what you are talking about. (Worse yet is the situation where grantseekers follow your advice because they presume that you have expertise you just do not possess.) Give advice sparingly, if at all. And if you do offer your insights, be very sure that you speak from a solid base of knowledge.

Are You Arrogant?

A well-respected scholar and head of an independent think tank spent almost 20 minutes with me angrily describing an experience with program officers at another foundation. The grantseeker and other staff members had spent more than a year in dialogue with the foundation, responding to comments and questions and recasting the proposal to fit the foundation's requirements, only to be told that morning that funding would not be forthcoming because the "foundation's guidelines were changing." The organization's staff members had spent time and money working on the proposal in response to the foundation's demands, sending new drafts, incurring travel expenses to visit the foundation, not to mention the emotional investment of expectations. As the nonprofit executive explained, it would have been better of the foundation had just said "no" to begin with.

Manion, Gerri. "Are You Arrogant?" *Foundation News & Commentary*, July/August 1997, p. 24.

Gerri Manion is a Program Officer, Special Projects, at the Carnegie Corporation in New York City.

Occupational Hazard 3: Other people's expectations.

To many nonprofits, the method and manner by which foundations make their decisions appears mysterious, if not downright mystical. Given this state of confusion, coupled with the ferocious competition for grants, some organizations will reshape their goals and programs into an illogical pretzel in hopes of conforming to your desires. If your guidelines are loose, gauzy, allusive and imprecise, you are guaranteed that large numbers of nonprofits will contort themselves in this manner.

The scope of your authority to approve or deny grant requests can also prove a tricky area. At times, you may be charged with the power to make a final decision, although it is usually to deny a grant. More frequently, you occupy a middle position between the grantseekers and the decisionmakers—a hazardous posture in itself. You must shuttle information between parties, keeping your board informed of the nonprofit's plans and achievements, while relaying your board's intentions to the applicant. In the best situation, you are a broker of crucial information. In the worst, you are somebody caught in the middle. Be clear when communicating with grantseekers about the decisionmaking process. Let them know who makes the final decision and when to expect that decision.

Nonprofit expectations also rise in accordance with the amount of time between the submission of a proposal and the date you finally respond. That does not mean you must render an immediate decision to every proposal crossing your desk. But do not allow weeks to pass before you let the applicant know when your full internal review process will conclude. Frequent contact will also raise the grantseeker's expectations, whether each encounter strengthens or erodes your interest. Consider the plight of the applicant whose hopes are pinned on your fateful decision. Be swift, timely, considerate. Also review your guidelines frequently and take the advice of grantseekers about how to improve them.

Occupational Hazard 4: Isolation.

As the months and then years pass, and you gather experience and expertise in your job, you will become more and more a denizen of the foundation world and less an actor of the nonprofit service sector that may have spawned you. As a result, you will no longer be privy to the same kind of information; the background music of many nonprofit projects, places and people will fade from your ears. Lodged in the rarified domain of money and power, you may find yourself starving for fresh insights, perspectives, a sense of the street. You can get what you need, but you will have to be sufficiently disciplined to extricate yourself from the comfort of your office and step out into the world of nonprofit action. Visit new programs; converse with former colleagues; read books, articles and studies to stay abreast of developments within your foundation's areas of interest. Take very seriously your duty not to become a philanthropic dinosaur.

Over time, you may also get the sense that the world is passing you by—or at least, you will notice an awful lot of new faces showing up at your door. That is because employment in the nonprofit sector is exceedingly volatile. According to several recent surveys, the tenure of nonprofit executives has been steadily declining. At present, we can expect a nonprofit executive director to stay on the job for an average of three years.[2] This sector-wide instability has implications for your own work. Most pointedly, you will find yourself frequently apprising new executive directors about the aims and policies of your foundation. In doing so, you may grow impatient, frustrated, bored. Be aware of this danger and strive to make your contact with new grantseekers an opportunity for fresh mutual exchange. Try always to learn something about their history, their organization, the field at large. Look for opportunities for exchange with colleagues in the funding community. Learn from their experiences, explore their perspectives on issues you have been dealing with. You may be surprised to find a rich array of approaches modeled for you. You may even find a partner to share your explorations.

Occupational Hazard 5: A workload that can bury you.

By definition, your job supports a crushing weight. Everybody wants something from you and they are willing to take as much time as you will give. Oftentimes, you will feel pulled between the never-ending demands of your board and your grantees. To complicate matters, the more conscientiously you dispatch your duties, the more opportunities will arise for further achievement and the cycle of endless effort renews itself. (There are always more programs to learn about, changing needs that must be reassessed, planning, convening or background reading to complete.) In short, your work lacks finality and closure. There is not a day when you can raise your hands to heaven and proclaim, "There, we did it, job accomplished."

You need to accept the hard truth that foundation work (like work in any other field or profession) is never done. But that does not mean you should dig yourself into an early grave or regard a constant level of frustration as anything but pathological. One guard against this hazard is the cultivation of excellent time management skills. Read the best books in this field; sign up for training. To serve your various constituencies with rigor and zeal, you must be able to set priorities and juggle myriad tasks so that you can feel sane, secure and satisfied on the job.

---

[2] Thomas, Jim. *Too Many Alligators*, Support Center for Nonprofit Management, October 1997. Wolfred, Timothy. *Leadership Lost: A Study of Executive Director Tenure & Experience*, Support Center for Nonprofit Management, March 1998.

Be strategic in the use of your time. Set priorities and, whenever possible, write them down. Strive for an alignment of your vision, strategies, systems and tasks precisely as you encourage grantseekers to do. Do not always respond to the squeaky wheel. Cultivate your capacity for making difficult decisions. Actively seek the advice of colleagues, experts *and* grantseekers.

Occupational Hazard 6: The curse of unintended consequences.

Grantmakers are frequently asked to intervene in complex systems, such as public education, healthcare delivery or conservation efforts. In doing so, they may help solve one problem only to exacerbate or create others. Think, for example, about how our nation's failed public housing programs of the 1960s were based on good intentions bolstered by presumptive logic about maintaining urban areas through new high-rise construction. It was simply not foreseen that large-scale public housing would actually destroy community and replace it with unlivable domains of crime and violence: concrete failures of public policy.

Grantmaking with the intention of systemic change is a decisive break with traditional notions of "charity" that once characterized philanthropy. Funding in pursuit of change demands clarity about ultimate ends and credible evidence that the visionary improvements of today will not transform themselves into the equivalent of hulking housing project failures of the future. In considering our potential for precipitating damage as well as good, we might remember that interventions in complex organizations are likely to produce untoward results unless the system is thoroughly understood. For this reason, we should proceed cautiously with any visionary project that intercedes in complex systems. In short, we must embrace a "do no harm" philosophy by cautiously endorsing any changes that could prove irreversible. The results of our interventions, whether a success or a failure, may take years or even decades to surface.

Special Opportunities

Lest your job begins to sound like an endless road of travail and hazard, let us not forget the unique advantages that will also come your way.

To begin, you will discover that you now enjoy widely expanded access. The money and power that create personal obstacles also generate extraordinary opportunities in terms of professional contacts. Key individuals and institutions in your community now relate to you as a peer. Staff people at larger, more established foundations embrace you as a colleague. The mayor's office, or even the mayor, returns your phone calls with alacrity. Your ability to get in the door and make your case has been magnified by a colossal factor.

Of course, the performance of your foundation and your professional reputation will determine over time whether these doors remain open. But from the start, you will enjoy the good will of many people who genuinely want to further your development as a grantmaker.

Beyond access and influence, you will find that your new role can also aid your education. If you need to learn something about a particular field, organization or individual, knowledgeable people will now gladly help to inform you. By sustaining your curiosity and willingness to learn, you will guarantee that you almost never have to operate from a position of ignorance.

The other great boon of foundation work is leverage. As a grantmaker, you now have the ability to bring powerful people and organizations to the table in order to solve important problems through collaborative effort. This can take place in several different ways.

To begin, your financial support of a project can be used to elicit the participation of other funders: A phone call from you to a colleague at another foundation may reap immediate results, while a nonprofit's pleas to the same person can go unanswered. (Your support speaks volumes to other funders.) Indeed, if yours is a respected institution with a strong public profile, your presence cannot be ignored. You may even be able to broker collaborations among business, government and the nonprofit sector without committing a single dollar from your foundation's grants budget. Savvy community leaders recognize that your foundation or corporate giving program is in business for the long haul.

Of course, you are not the only person with leveraging power. Your peers will also be trying to leverage you. Just remember: Leverage is not about shuffling the deck of personal favors. Rather, it is a means of concentrating appropriate resources, serving as a catalyst to solve important problems and galvanizing critical and substantial support for credible programs. Over time, you will relax into the rhythm of give-and-take.

Setting Your Course
GUIDELINES FOR EVERYBODY

All foundations and corporate giving programs need to debate, formulate, publish and disseminate their program guidelines. If they neglect to do so, the consequences will be borne by you, the staff, in the form of a constant barrage of irrelevant, time-wasting proposals.

Guidelines inform grant applicants about what your foundation hopes to accomplish. They illuminate the projects, proposals and organizations you aspire to assist, and conversely, point to what lies outside your interests. They are the most practical manifestation of the intent of the founders and the policies of the governing board.

Why is this public declaration necessary? It saves everybody time and effort.

If your foundation is exclusively concerned with child welfare projects, but fails to publicize this fact, then you are guaranteed to receive regular requests for museum acquisitions, senior housing ventures, ecological research in Brazil's rain forest and everything else under the nonprofit sun. You already have enough to do without adding another ultimately unproductive cycle of perusal and refusal. Likewise, nonprofits should devote their energies to activities that enjoy a genuine chance of achieving results.

By clarifying your foundation's aims and preferences, you will also find it easier to separate proposals that warrant a closer reading from those that can be immediately denied. Some proposals might even be returned to sender with a recommendation attached to pursue another funder whose guidelines fit better with the applicant's plans.

Guidelines also serve as a tool for nonprofits as they focus their thinking about funding aims. Guidelines establish reasonable expectations, helping applicants to realistically estimate their fundraising opportunities. As important, good guidelines document changes in your interests and provide as much specificity as possible about program emphases. For example, they should enable applicants from the youth service field to distinguish between foundations that specialize in direct services, research or organizational development.

Of course, all of these statements hinge on the expectation that your guidelines will be clearly written and adhered to by your board. As many nonprofit applicants will tell you, not all foundations' guidelines are clear or specific.

Some foundations opt for that famous phrase, "Dedicated to general welfare." In a practical sense, this really is not a guideline. It is a declaration of the board's refusal to grapple with its mission, its reluctance to set goals and establish priorities. Nevertheless, a very general statement of this kind may be the necessary starting place for your foundation. It may even be sufficient if your geographic area is focused and narrow. But generally, good guidelines take time, hard work and the patient carpentry of successive drafts. In the process of crafting more specific guidelines, your board may confront the tensions and contradictions that have heretofore resided beneath the surface of the foundation operations for decades. Indeed, the formulation of guidelines probably should stimulate spirited debate.

What should your guidelines contain?

- A statement of purpose, declaring in broad terms the goal of your grantmaking program.
- An indication of your foundation's fields of interest characterized in general, familiar terms, such as housing, the arts, education, the environment.
- The geographical range in which you will consider funding, thereby indicating whether you will review proposals exclusively from your city, county, region, state, nation or the entire world.
- A brief description of your decisionmaking process, including dates for proposal submission and review.
- Declarations of anything you definitely will not fund, such as building construction, endowments or out-of-state programs.
- Examples of grants that you have previously awarded.
- Any special interests or emphases not otherwise indicated in the statement of purpose.
- The typical dollar range of your grants.
- How to proceed with an application: what to include and what *not* to include with the request.
- Name and contact information of the person in charge of reviewing proposals.
- The guidelines' publication date.

Once the guidelines are approved by the board, your job is still not over. You must decide how to make them available and easily accessible to grantseekers. Many avenues are available and multiple approaches may be advisable: Web sites, printed brochures, even face-to-face discussions with potential applicants. At least annually, you should review the guidelines and ask yourself if they honestly reflect your board's recent history of grantmaking. If you have been receiving a large number of proposals outside your program interests, then you should check to see if your guidelines are sending the wrong message. Or if you have persistently awarded grants outside your declared aims, you and your board should strive to reconcile the guidelines with your actual philanthropic practice.

It Takes Time

GROWING INTO THE JOB

Soon you will learn what is required of you on the job. You will pick up new skills. You will set goals for yourself and make progress toward achieving them. With time, you will become increasingly effective in every aspect of your job.

Time: That is what it takes to grow into your job. Time coupled with effort.

In your first months on the job, you might take the opportunity to meet with your grantees. You can ask them the questions that you might have been struggling to answer on your own and in the process open up the lines of communication.

- What are some things that I need to learn about your organization, your field, the nonprofit sector?
- Is there anything in our guidelines that is not clear, something that should be excluded or included?
- What in your experience constitutes a successful site visit? A good grant proposal? An effective collaboration between a nonprofit and a foundation?
- From your perspective, what are the key issues and challenges grantmakers and grantseekers will face in the coming years?

Over time, you may want to experiment with various grantmaking strategies. You might measure the conventional responsive approach (in which you wait for the proposals to pour into your office and then take action) with an orientation that is decidedly proactive. You and your board will decide what kinds of efforts you most want to fund and then you will comb the nonprofit sector to find them.

You may want to cluster your grants, reviewing at one time all the proposals dealing with a single issue; proposals originating from particular geographical area; or proposals that address an area of special interest to your foundation.

Gradually, you will become a minor expert in more subjects than you thought possible. You will learn what a really good organization looks like—the odd rumblings of its inner operations. You will learn what constitutes a good proposal. The feel of how things really work in the nonprofit sector. You will learn that in the foundation world, there is never just one way to achieve great things. You will witness the accomplishments and false starts of your colleagues. You will learn from their example, too.

Your own journey is just beginning. It can prove spectacularly interesting, rewarding in ways you have never before experienced. Gratifying on a grand-scale and a deeply personal level. It all depends on your commitment and your willingness to grow into the job over time.

CHAPTER 2

Panning for Gold

How to Review Grant Proposals

During the course of your professional life, you will read hundreds, even thousands of grant proposals. The skill you bring to this task will significantly determine your giving program's success at advancing its mission and helping the nonprofit sector to aid our society in every imaginable way.

Of course, nobody starts out in the funding world as a deft and canny reviewer of grant proposals. That comes only with time and the enlightening (if occasionally exhausting) experience of scanning, studying, analyzing, questioning, summarizing and digesting a huge number proposals whose quality will undoubtedly range from the sleep-inducing to the sublime.

But let us start at the beginning.

What is a grant proposal, and why do we use it? Think of a grant proposal as a prospectus for an investment opportunity. In this case, the return on investment that you are seeking is not monetary profit, but public benefit.

A serviceable proposal details one of society's standing needs or problems. It outlines an organizational strategy for addressing the problem and justifies the methods. The proposal indicates who will handle each important task, for what duration and at what cost. Like a prospectus for a new business, the grant proposal must convince you that the organization is sound and its plans are likely to achieve its intended goals.

Assuming the proposal fits your guidelines, it is your job to determine whether the venture enjoys a fair chance of success and, as important, whether it belongs in your foundation's diverse portfolio of investments in the common good.

Opportunities for Everybody

WHY PROPOSALS MAKE SENSE

For grantmakers, the proposal format has several obvious benefits. First, it reinforces your foundation's own need to be clear about its funding goals. You cannot accept proposals from organizations engaged in all varieties of endeavor from every corner of the world. Should you try, you will inevitably flood your foundation with paper and drown the staff in a sea of ungratifiable expectations. Instead, you and your board must forthrightly confront the matter of limits by establishing guidelines for your grantmaking. By declaring your intention to entertain proposals of one sort and not another, your foundation or giving program will itself gain clarity, definition and identity.

Beyond tightening up your own operations, the proposal offers the most efficient means of quickly learning about a potential grantee's current programs, future plans, past accomplishments. This informed introduction can serve as an embarkation point for additional discussion, site visits, deeper investigations that can lead to collaboration. In fact, the proposal often signals the beginning, not the culmination of a relationship between grantmaker and grantseeker.

Grantmakers, however, are not the only ones to benefit from the proposal process. When prepared with care, deliberation and integrity, the arduous task of proposal writing can also deliver substantial benefits to organizations seeking grants.

Proposal writing can make organizations take a hard look at their programs and goals. The process can clarify basic organizational assumptions by rendering once-vague thoughts into resonant prose. It can compel staff and board to order their priorities and firm-up plans, while drawing together key people to forge new working alliances within the organization or with other agencies. It may even result in clarification of the organization's mission, an extremely healthy process that is too often bypassed in the bustle of daily labors. Finally, a growing file of well-crafted proposals can add to the organizational memory by documenting the plans, programs and thinking that has characterized efforts down through the years.

Of course, we are talking here about an ideal situation in which organizations submit well-wrought proposals born of assiduous planning and careful review. Unfortunately, not all proposal writers will excel at their job. At worst, they will offer incoherent summaries of half-baked ideas, or they will set out on a fishing expedition, dangling before you a variety of glittery, but ill-conceived programs in an attempt to merely attract funding. These lackadaisical efforts waste everybody's time. In the end, organizations lose on two counts: You will not fund them and they will learn nothing from the process.

Most proposals fall somewhere in the middle. They will introduce you to an interesting organization committed to a just cause through a variety of serviceable means. But the question remains: Is this particular project right for your foundation?

Reading the Proposal

Try to be mindful that a well-written proposal does not automatically mean you have discovered the perfect program. Nor does a poorly-written proposal necessarily indicate an unfundable organization. If it only were otherwise, the grant review process would prove a snap. In truth, the evaluation of proposals is rife with paradox and complication.

Yet you should find it relatively easy to begin your work if these three conditions pertain:

- Your foundation or giving program's priorities are clear, and you have provided useful guidelines to help applicants present their best case.
- The applicants have studied the guidelines and followed them.
- You have set aside sufficient uninterrupted quiet time to read the proposals.

Clearly, the first condition is a responsibility you share with your board of directors. If you collectively neglect this task, you will simply buy days, weeks and months of wasted hours spent poring over irrelevant applications. Even if you do resolutely order your priorities and painstakingly prepare your guidelines, you will still be bothered now and then by inappropriate proposals. A grantseeker will ask you to underwrite the construction costs of their new offices when the guidelines are clear that your foundation does not fund building campaigns, or a Florida-based organization will seek support when your foundation only funds programs in Michigan. The point is to limit the number of errant applications heading your way and save everybody time and energy.

Beyond offering clear direction to grantseekers about funding goals and requirements, you cannot ensure the submission of good proposals. It is largely up to the applicants to rise to the challenge—the second condition.

The third condition, so deceptive in its simplicity, is the one that most frequently haunts program officers. Experienced grantmakers routinely observe that it is very difficult to carve out enough free time to give their proposals the attention they deserve. Yet in this constant struggle over time, you must prevail. Proposal reading is demanding work: Endeavor always to give it your undivided attention.

The Virtues of Scanning

You need not, however, give every proposal the same degree of attention—at least not initially. Try on a regular basis, perhaps weekly, to scan the proposals that have recently landed upon your desk.

Look for the name of the organization and the person who signed the letter of introduction. Try to determine why the proposal was sent your way. Was it referred by a colleague? Is the applicant following up on a previous discussion with you? Is there any reason why you must take action immediately?

If the request is urgent, you might sit down and read the proposal right away and formulate your funding recommendation. If the proposal obviously does not fit your guidelines, you can dispatch it immediately by writing the applicant a decline letter.

Saying No and Feeling (sort-of) O.K. about It

This book is about making grants, connecting resources to feasible and practical approaches for making our world a better place. It is about the steps and stages of a grantmaker's work in getting to the message all grantseekers want to hear: "We are pleased to offer support…"

But we must also face the fact that a part of the daily reality of making grants is turning down many worthy requests. In fact, most of us turn down many more grant requests than we are able to recommend for support. So, how do you say no responsibly and constructively?

OUTSIDE GUIDELINES

The easiest requests to deny are the ones that clearly do not fit with your foundation's current guidelines or funding priorities. A worthy request from a senior center submitted to a corporate giving program that is focused exclusively on the arts is easy to deal with. In such a case, the grantmaker's job is to respond quickly so that the applicant's expectations are not unnecessarily inflated. The sooner you deliver the news that your foundation or giving program cannot offer the sought for support, the better. It allows the applicant to use the time to locate other more likely sources of support for its work.

If you are impressed or intrigued by the proposal, you may be able to connect the applicant with a funder who would be more likely support the request. If you do succeed at this sort of matchmaking, it can be very gratifying for all involved, but be sensitive about when (and how often) you send unsuccessful grant applicants to a colleague at another foundation. Remember that you are increasing your colleague's workload. You may also be wasting a grantseeker's time unless there is a reasonable hope of success in securing funds. As a courtesy, you may want to check with your funder colleagues before you refer a grantseeker to them.

MANY FINE PROPOSALS

More difficult, but still straightforward, are the requests that technically fit the guidelines but where the competitiveness of the grant process will not allow for all applications to succeed. Here in the guidelines it is essential for you—the grantmaker—to be clear about the criteria for making decisions to fund or to deny. Are you looking for innovative approaches and start-up efforts, or are you committed to supporting the tried and true efforts of a few exemplary organizations? It may even be helpful to let the applicant know what their chances of success are. If you are only able to support one request in ten, it is easier to hear the news and harder to see it as a personal failure.

A GREAT IDEA, BUT…

You face another kind of dilemma when you encounter a proposal that simply cannot be funded as written, but hints at a promising approach in need of further development. In such a case, you must decide how much time to invest in coaching the grantseeker so that they can submit a more competitive proposal next time. Grantees would like a complete description of all of the reasons you are denying this proposal. This, they feel, would allow them a better opportunity to correct misconceptions, explain things differently, provide additional information or at least learn what is wrong and why they failed. Remember that almost any communication from you will increase a grantseeker's hopes. Be judicious and specific when inviting a new proposal—and be honest with the grantseeker about the real potential for success if he or she puts in the extra effort a new proposal will require.

NO MEANS NO

Finally, there is the case of the persistent grantseeker who will not accept "no" for an answer. John Q. Grantseeker calls for an explanation of your reasons for denying the request. He demands reconsideration; he pleads for advice and instructions for resubmitting. You feel sympathetic, but you know that there is nothing this grantseeker can do to make his proposal competitive. In this case, a firm and brief response is needed. Do not send a mixed message by engaging in long conversations or helping the grantseeker to rewrite his proposal. Remember that if you are to succeed in your job, you must invest most—if not all—of your time working with grantseekers who have the potential to become grantees.

Your overall goal is to create a speedy in-and-out box so that you never have a mountain of proposals sitting on your desk. In clearing away both the urgent and the irrelevant, you will afford yourself more time to study most proposals that fall somewhere in between.

Reading Closely

Reviewing grant applications would be far easier if you dealt with only ten proposals each year. But most program officers find their desks piled high annually with scores of proposals, if not hundreds. The sheer magnitude of the task adds another dimension to your work. Indeed, it is an accomplishment of the first order to meet this challenge with a graceful balance of judgement, intuition, curiosity, zeal and a healthy dose of skepticism.

In most foundations, grantmaking spans a dizzying range of pursuits. Education, the environment, welfare reform, urban reclamation, human rights, animal rights, the justice system—nobody can possibly claim expertise in all of these fields. Yet over time, you will need to become at least conversant with every area your foundation considers funding. To a significant degree, your continuing education begins—and proceeds throughout your career—with reading and re-reading grant proposals that inform you of the context, controversies, problems and best practices in numerous fields.

With all that said, there are several ways for you to make the process more comfortable and productive.

First, when it is time to sit down and study the proposals that warrant careful consideration, make certain once again that you have allotted sufficient time to work without interruptions. Redirect your phone calls. Schedule meetings for other days. Then begin to read slowly, concentrating on the document as though it was a contract whose terms and stipulations will seriously affect your future (as, indeed, they may).

As you read, take notes in the margins of the proposal or on a separate pad of paper. As questions arise, jot them down. Some questions will probably be answered further along in the text. If they are not, consign them to a more permanent list for further follow-up.

Throughout your reading, you should search for these signal virtues:

- **Credibility.** The proposal will indicate in numerous ways whether the organization appears to be a reliable potential grantee. Ask yourself: Does the organization know what it wants to accomplish? What is the evidence that the organization is currently achieving its goals? What kind of reputation does the group enjoy within its community and beyond?

- **Capability.** Your foundation is not merely in the business of supporting good ideas; you are also investing in people who can turn these ideas into reality, as well as an organization that has the structure and systems in place to achieve its goals. What skills do the organization's staff and board bring to the project? Are they relevant to the project's aims? Has the organization succeeded in similar endeavors of equal size and scale to what they are now proposing? In short, you want to find out if the staff and board of the applicant organization can carry out the project or program effectively. (Some foundations appreciate attachments, such as press clippings and staff biographies as evidence of both credibility and capability.)

- **Feasibility.** You will be trying to determine whether the proposal is advancing a worthwhile project built upon a good idea that can be successfully implemented by the sponsoring organization. This question of feasibility naturally touches upon both credibility and capability; an uncredible, incapable organization is not the logical source of exemplary work. But you must also consider the project on its own terms, apart from the sponsoring organization. Simply put: Can it be done? You will need to consult the budget to make certain that the organization has allocated sufficient resources to execute the various tasks and strategies described in the proposal. (See chapter 4.)

- **Importance.** Beyond the very sensible question of can and will a project be completed, you will necessarily ask yourself: Should it be done? Is the project significant? Is there evidence that the proposal will trigger action or work that the community wants? Will it make a difference in the community it purports to aid or resolve the issue it addresses? Given your other opportunities for funding, is it the right one to support at this time?

Questions to Ask When Reading the Proposal

Joel Orosz, of the W. K. Kellogg Foundation, has sagely observed that there are really only four kinds of proposals:[3]

- Good idea, good proposal
- Good idea, bad proposal
- Bad idea, good proposal
- Bad idea, bad proposal

---

[3] Orosz, Joel. "Proposals: How to Separate the Good, Bad, and the Ugly—12 Principles," a speech presented during the Council of Michigan Foundations' 23rd Annual Conference, 1995. W. K. Kellogg Foundation.

The first and last categories are easy to handle. (Reject the latter outright; seriously consider the former.) It is the other two kinds of imperfect, yet promising applications that will prove most nettlesome and numerous.

To fully grasp the virtues and liabilities of any proposal, and to make an accurate judgement about credibility, capability, feasibility and importance, it will help to focus on the questions in the Appendix to Chapter 2. Each question is easy to ask and very challenging to answer, both for the proposal writer and the reviewer.

A failure to glean satisfactory answers to all of these questions from reading a proposal should not immediately prompt you to deny the request. The lack of information may rather indicate your need to turn to other sources (see chapter 3). In addition, not every question is pertinent to every proposal.

Looking for Trouble
COMMON PROPOSAL PROBLEMS

Consistency and clarity are the hallmarks of excellent proposals. In the best of all possible worlds, you will encounter proposals that address a genuine need with a program based on realistic expectations and imaginative ideas. Capable people committed to the project's success and backed up by a board that comprehends and supports the organization's overall mission will staff the organization. Administrators will have allocated sufficient time, money and personnel to accomplishing the project's measurable goals. They will chart the project's continuing progress, providing a clear, frank evaluation upon its completion.

Unfortunately, most proposals do not match this ideal. It is this realm of imperfect proposals that makes your work so demanding.

You will find that through inexperience or lack of sophistication in proposal writing, grantseekers most commonly err through omission.

- **Financial information**, including the project budget, potential sources of income, annual organizational budget or audit, is missing, incomplete or inadequately rendered.
- **Board lists** fail to include affiliations, professional skills or contact numbers.
- **Evaluation plans** are sketchy or absent.
- **Staff biographies** fail to correlate past experience to the skills needed to complete the project.
- **Knowledge of best practices** is not apparent in the narrative, thereby failing to demonstrate the staff's grasp of the field or their own organization's experience.
- **Budget expenditures** are not justified, suggesting that the applicant may be attempting to plug holes in the organization's leaky operating budget.
- **Explanations of rapid staff turnover** or recent changes in leadership remain unexplained, raising questions about organizational continuity, direction and morale.
- **Little discussion of external trends** or internal organizational challenges that may affect the chances of success.

Eight Qualities of Exemplary Proposals

1. **Energy**. The proposal bristles with enthusiasm, urgency, passion. It suggests a group of people who can barely contain their eagerness to begin working. As a reader, you find yourself inspired and excited by their plans.

2. **Expertise**. The proposal's authors know what they are talking about. Their plans reflect a deep understanding of the problem they are addressing. They are aware of similar efforts that have been undertaken in the past. Their theoretical knowledge is tempered by time-tested experience in the field. They inform their practice with solid theory and continue their own professional development despite the demands of their daily work.

3. **Commitment**. The proposal reflects the organization's genuine priorities rather than being one of many programs it is currently juggling. The grantseekers demonstrate their willingness to invest their own unrestricted resources in the project. Rather than moving on to a new endeavor in the near future, the organization is committed to continuing the project.

4. **Clarity**. The proposal is clear about what the organization wants to do, why it is important and how it will be carried out and evaluated.

5. **Collaboration**. The grantseeker has formed alliances with other organizations to advance their mutual goals. The people served by the proposed project have participated in its planning. All involved parties appear more interested in getting results than carving out turf.

6. **Benefits**. The organization is less concerned with underwriting its own needs than improving society. The project's goals are indisputably worth striving for and the target group is appropriate.

7. **Comprehensiveness**. The problem's complexity is matched by the sophistication of its proposed solution. The grantseekers' thinking reflects a comprehensive strategy, rather than a piecemeal approach.

8. **Effectiveness**. A well-designed, ongoing evaluation reflects the group's commitment to getting results. The project has the potential for achieving a wider impact if it is replicated elsewhere in the future.

Keep in mind that applicants will be striving to put their best foot forward. Do not expect them to stress the obstacles to their success or their own implacable organizational difficulties. Give them the benefit of the doubt, then ask for whatever additional information you may need in order to make an informed decision.

When the Truth Lies Elsewhere

GETTING BEYOND WORDS

When you do encounter an interesting proposal promoting a worthy idea, you should not assume that your job is nearing completion. Actually, it is just beginning.

Let us say you have reviewed a proposal submitted by a long-established organization that rings out with commitment and enthusiasm, while passionately establishing a critical need that can be addressed by the project's logically outlined strategies. Now you must ask: Do these qualities characterize the entire organization or are they the product of skillful grantwriting and perhaps a professional grantwriter?

On the other hand, when you read a muddled proposal from a grassroots organization or start-up venture—unable to benefit from the services of a professional development officer or fundraising consultant—you may need to look at the question from the opposite direction. Ask yourself: Is a valuable effort being undersold because of the organization's lack of an articulate advocate? Does an unsophisticated approach to organizational charts, financial statements and budgets reflect an inept effort or a worthwhile venture at an early stage of development?

Reviewing proposals is not like judging an essay contest. Whether a proposal is eloquent or incoherent, you will still need to burrow underneath the prose to acquire a genuine sense of organizational reality. Do not ever entirely trust what you find on paper. The proposal is a very important indicator of an organization's aims, plans and accomplishments, but it can never tell the whole story.

If you are dealing with an agency that has a long history with your founda-

Mistakes You Might Make While Reading Proposals

- **Perfectionism**. No proposal seems adequate. You feel impatient and beleaguered. (Why can't applicants think and write better? Why are you always burdened by insufficient efforts?) But we do not live in a perfect world; why should you expect to encounter consistently perfect proposals? Stop reading and do something different. Return to your proposal review when you are in a more empathic and realistic frame of mind.

- **Credulousness**. For whatever reason—fatigue, lack of knowledge, a longing to suspend your skepticism for just a moment—you have taken the proposal at face value. That might be understandable if you are dealing with an organization whose past collaborations with your foundation have proven faultless. Nevertheless, retain your skepticism. In moderate doses, it is your friend.

- **Personal charm**. You genuinely like the applicants: They are bright, good-intentioned, hard-working. Leadership in the field is rare and should be nurtured. Their proposal is lousy, yet you want to fund it anyway. This temptation of intimacy is a human enough failing. Maybe you have been unduly impressed by the director's longstanding reputation. Pull back and remember: The best people do not try to sell a poor program to their funders. Consider working with the applicants. Tell them what is missing in the proposal and then ask them to try again.

- **Institutional weight**. You are inclined to support an institution because of its past performance. But organizations change, and not always for the better. You need to maintain a consistent review standard for every group, large and small, renowned and unknown.

- **Hurry and fatigue**. You have too many tasks to accomplish. You speed through the proposals without fully digesting their content and implication. You wear yourself out by reading too many proposals at one time. You rely on someone else's opinion, feeling that if he or she has looked into this project you should not spend your time on it. Your critical faculties have faded: You need a break.

Chapter 2: Panning for Gold

tion, you can begin to plumb the depths of organizational life by digging into your own files. Consult their final reports to determine whether the organization actually has performed as promised in the past. Refresh your memory about your foundation's prior relationship with the organization and ask whether it bears repeating.

If you have not previously worked with the group, you can consult other funders who have. Ask them to talk frankly about their experience. Apply the same rigor to this task as you would when following up the references of a job applicant for a key position inside your organization. In truth, you are embarking on a kind of partnership that demands a clear-eyed appraisal of your potential grantee's strengths and weaknesses.

Help for Hire

OUTSIDE REVIEWERS AND ADVISORS

At times you may find yourself needing help in evaluating a proposal. Assistance can come in several forms: coworkers at your foundation, colleagues working at other foundations or funding agencies, or experts outside the field of philanthropy, such as community leaders or scholars.

If you do not have collegial contacts, then the request for help may be a good first step in building them.

Let us say your foundation or corporate giving program has recently decided to concentrate on child development, an area in which you have no previous experience. Over time, you will need to familiarize yourself with the field's key issues and your foundation's grantmaking history. More immediately, you must grapple with the applications piling up on your desk. This is a perfect moment to bundle up some of your proposals and ship them off to an outside expert.

Of course, you will be looking for a good deal more from the expert than a simple approval or rejection of each proposal. You can benefit most by studying the experts' assessment: First, by reading his or her report on each proposal, and then by engaging in a frank conversation about the decisionmaking process. The next time a batch of similar proposals arrives, you will be better prepared to evaluate them yourself.

What should you be looking for in an outside expert?

- Personal experience in running or designing programs like the ones you are reviewing.
- The ability to analyze complicated situations and write up findings in a clear and succinct manner.
- Perspective as a policymaker in the field, or the proper educational credentials and an abiding, scholarly interest in the area.
- Enough time to review the proposals and return them to you when you need them.

Whomever you select, you will want to avoid any possible conflict of interest. Stay clear of people directly connected to organizations seeking funding. Even if they can complete the job effectively, you may face the appearance of impropriety, which can be as destructive as the thing itself.

When you have a personal relationship with an applicant, the situation may also become sticky. In these cases, consider an outside reviewer as a complement to your own reading. Regional Associations of Grantmakers (RAGs) are good resources for referrals. (See Appendix to Chapter 1.)

When Talk Is Not Cheap

COMMUNICATING WITH APPLICANTS DURING THE REVIEW PROCESS

Grantseekers and grantmakers cannot possibly share the same point of view. Grantseekers are concerned with their own institution. Their attention focuses on the one proposal they have dispatched to your foundation. On the other hand, many grantmakers see hundreds of proposals each and every month. Their outlook is necessarily broader, although not necessarily as deep.

This inevitable difference sometimes complicates communication. Grantseekers long to hear a hint of encouragement in your voice, even when you are telling them why you cannot possibly fund their project. They may regard any suggestions you make as a directive linked to future funding. They may not hear you at all, their ears clogged by the implications of your approval or refusal to fund their project.

Strive to keep conversations with grantseekers

- **Practical.** Let them know if you want to see additional information or require clarifications on any part of their proposal.

- **Informative.** The most common inquiry you will receive from applicants after they have submitted a proposal: When will we hear from you about your decision? It is only fair that applicants be apprised of the timing of your review process and kept informed of any unusual delays. It is also of benefit to both grantseeker and grantmaker to be clear about the steps and stages of the grant review process.

- **Uncommitted.** Do not make promises you cannot keep.

Unless you can guarantee that your funding recommendations will be adopted, wait until your board has taken action before passing along the news to grantseekers. If you have to retract a promise of funding, it will make your foundation appear indecisive, while you look less than competent. Even worse, it suggests that you and your board are in conflict over funding priorities. Grantseekers will have nowhere to turn, having lost faith in you both. Keep in mind that you generally do not have the power to approve grants; you only have the power to deny because your negative response will most likely halt the application before it ever reaches your board. Strive for truthfulness and transparency in your relationship with the grantseeker.

Getting Better All the Time

HOW TO IMPROVE YOUR PROPOSAL REVIEWING SKILLS

Despite all the challenges, you will certainly sharpen your proposal-reviewing skills as your career progresses. Reading proposals with care and concentration demands strength, endurance, flexibility; it will keep you fit on the job. You can, however, speed up the development of your reviewing skills if you are willing to take some extra effort.

To begin, try to make the review process as interactive as possible. Do not merely scan the words on the page. Speak back to each proposal; try to engage yourself in a conversation in which you point out the proposal's virtues and shortcomings. Beyond making judgements about fitness for funding, formulate your own criteria for excellence as you might cultivate a personal aesthetic for viewing art or listening to music. The point here is to turn proposal reviewing into a profoundly conscious act.

Take care to vary the kinds of proposals you review. Notice the ways that different kinds of organizations approach the proposal writing process. Do artists and scientists conceive of their projects in opposing or complementary ways? What values and preconceptions underlie the proposals submitted by educators, by environmentalists, by groups involved with international development? Precisely what is the meaning of the jargon indulged in by various constituencies and organizations?

Rely on your colleagues for advice. Ask staff people at other foundations to forward their own examples of exemplary proposals. Note the variance from your own maturing standards. Contrast the values celebrated by your colleagues. Engage other foundation professionals and your nonprofit collaborators in an ongoing discussion about what constitutes a good proposal. Stay open to other people's ideas. And keep reading.

CHAPTER 3

Conducting Site Visits and Interviews

A Guide for Program Officers

Few tasks in the foundation world prove as interesting, rewarding and exhilarating as the site visit.

Site visits can lift your spirits and enliven your day by reminding you precisely why you chose to work in the foundation world. They invite you to compare plans with accomplishments, the ideal with the real, the fundable with the feasible. By speaking in-person with grant applicants and surveying their operations, you can gather crucial information, add depth and texture to your funding recommendations, cultivate your professional skills and expand your knowledge of the extraordinarily diverse non-profit world.

Yet, while the benefits of site visits are potentially vast, the challenges also remain formidable. To start, how do you decide which applicants to visit? It all begins with the proposal.

When to Go

In most cases, the proposal will be your primary means of determining which organizations and projects enjoy sufficient potential to justify an in-depth, in-person site visit and interview.

Before scheduling any site visit, you should carefully review the proposal and ask yourself six basic questions:

1. Is the proposed project within our foundation's guidelines?
2. Does it describe a program or project that appears realistic and reasonably constructed?
3. Are skilled, committed, dependable people running the organization?
4. Will the project's success really make a difference in the world?
5. Do you have any important questions about the project that are not answered in the proposal?
6. Do you know enough about the organization, its managers and its proposed actions to make a recommendation without conducting a site visit?

Of course, these questions are not meant as exhaustive criteria for determining an organization's worth or a project's potential. They are simply guidelines suggesting when you should consider stepping through the door to learn more.

In short, they tell you whether your foundation might benefit from taking a longer, harder and more personal look at an organization, its plans, its programs and its people.

When to Stay Home

Of course, there are also plenty of good reasons not to take the time to conduct a site visit. Among the least defensible motivations:

- You or the applicant feel like "shooting the breeze" for an hour or so.
- You long to share your opinion and offer "expert" advice.
- You have not had an opportunity to read the organization's proposal; instead, you will drop by for the oral rendition.
- An old friend on the organization's board would really appreciate it if you could pay a short visit.
- You have time on your hands today; why not get out of the office for a break, even though there is really nothing to see or learn?

A foundation representative motivated by any of these flimsy rationales would be better off staying home. A site visit is not a trifling matter; it is a fundamental tool for conducting important research. Site visits raise the expectations and involve considerable preparation time on the part of the grantseeker. Justifiable site visits represent a crucial step in uniting a worthy applicant and a responsible foundation in their mutual effort to make the world better. Unjustifiable site visits waste the time of the grantmaker and the grantseeker.

Benefits of the Site Visit

Once you have wisely chosen an organization to visit, what benefits can you expect from your effort?

MEET THE PEOPLE

First, and perhaps most important, you will meet key staff and board members. These are the people responsible for implementing the project you have only read about. Through their proposal, the staff has asked you join them as collaborators; step one is getting acquainted. In the best of circumstances, your first site visit will mark the beginning of a long and fruitful working relationship. In the worst situations, it can prevent you from hitching your foundation's money and reputation to a venture that is creeping toward disaster.

In addition to speaking with the executive director and the project manager, you should also try to meet with at least one active board member, particularly in smaller nonprofits. After all, your grant will go directly into the organization's coffers. You should learn about the group's long-term commitment, durability and fiscal health by speaking with the individuals who are legally, financially and morally charged with its oversight and governance.

If at all possible, meet with the frontline staff who serve the clientele. In this way, you can determine whether the proposed project has the necessary depth of skills, knowledge and motivation to fulfill its promise, or whether the project's fate balances on the overloaded shoulders of the executive director.

LEARN MORE ABOUT THE ORGANIZATION AND ITS PROJECT

The best projects raise questions. Some questions—provoked by your careful reading of the proposal—can be answered quickly by the organization's knowledgeable people. Other matters may demand research, some consideration and another call or meeting at a later date.

In any case, the site visit stands as your chance to learn abundantly more than you knew when you read the proposal.

At the site visit, you can ask the staff and board to elaborate on their plans, goals and vision. With luck—and the proper management of the interview on your part—they will soon move beyond the standard fare of pleasant generalities to delve into the livelier, more invigorating issues that make their work important and interesting. You will become privy to the operational details and philosophical principles that characterize their field. You will glean some of the texture and turmoil that speaks to the deep truth of the organization, its project and its mission.

SEE BEYOND THE PROPOSAL

Some organizations are blessed with fluent, persuasive proposal writers on staff; other organizations hire them on a contract basis. In either case, you must learn to distinguish the rhetoric from reality, the promises from real potential.

This need is compounded by the fact that in most organizations the person writing a grant proposal is not the same person who will implement the project. As a result, misinformation may seep into the planning. The proposal may suffer from an inflated prose style that raises questions about its credibility. In fact, these conditions are so common that we probably should not characterize them as "problems"; it is nonprofit reality. Overanxious project planners frequently feel compelled to promise too much in pursuit of their grant. You can use your site visit to redirect responsibly the conversation toward more realistic goals and to avoid the mutually chafing bind of approving a grant that asks for more than can be delivered. Incremental progress is usually the order of the day.

On the other hand, some excellent organizations—particularly newcomers to the field—find themselves tongue-tied when they sit down to write about their efforts. A site visit can help you tease out qualities in a project that may not be visible in a disorganized or thinly argued grant proposal.

GAIN A SENSE OF PLACE

You should also open yourself up to acquiring a "feel" for the organization and its people. We are talking here about gut reactions, but something else, too. Look around: Is the space adequate? Is it well-organized or are files scattered everywhere? Does it feel "user-friendly?" On closer inspection, our "intuition" about people and places is often triggered by subtle clues. If the organization you are visiting feels rather "empty" or "slow," It may be due to the fact that you have not heard the phone ring all morning or noticed a single client walk through the door. ("When do things get moving around here?" you might want to ask, in the least provocative way possible.) On the other hand, if you encounter an organization that is jumping with purposeful activity, teeming with enthusiasm, determination, joy, then that is certainly worth noting, too.

ADVANCE PROFESSIONAL DEVELOPMENT

Site visits can also do you the enormous favor of extending your education in all the program areas that your foundation funds.

Remember, the very fact of your visit becomes part of what you see and what you experience. You are not just a visitor, you are an actor and you are cast in a starring role.

Remember, too, that the point of your visit is not to simply gather information. It should be seen as a sign of interest and respect whether or not your foundation makes a grant. For your site visit to be a success, except in the rarest of circumstances, the result should leave your hosts feeling appreciated, understood and proud of their work.

Thomas C. Layton, President
Wallace A. Gerbode Foundation

As a foundation executive or program officer, you simply cannot keep up with all the latest developments in juvenile justice, community economic development, the arts, education and the environment. That is asking too much of any one person. But you can take advantage of your position to conscientiously and persistently seek out information from experts dealing with the issues on a day-to-day basis: the leaders of the nonprofit organizations striving for your support. Learn from them; ask questions.

What are the trends you see coming? What should our foundation be looking at? What changes do you anticipate in your field? Are there ways in which people frequently misperceive your issue, your clients, your organization? How have you overcome the challenges that other agencies now face? Who else is doing good work in your field? What should I take special care to learn?

By talking with intelligent, well-informed nonprofit managers, workers and board members about their areas of expertise, as well as their individual projects, you can draw upon their collective experience to discreetly inform your own perspective. In the end, this kind of conscious, continuing education will make you a more effective foundation representative, which in turn will benefit everybody.

DETERMINE ACTUAL NEED

A site visit might also tell you whether an organization really needs your money. But beware: This kind of judgement can be fraught with paradox. A brisk, orderly, well-managed organization might point to a good bet for funding, or to a group that already has enough money to accomplish its goals.

Beyond the simple calculation to support or deny a funding request, the site visit can provide a basis for determining whether an organization needs as much money as it is requesting, or instead technical assistance to address organizational problems it might be overlooking.

PROVIDE HELPFUL ADVICE

Occasionally, you will stumble upon an opportunity to offer useful counsel. Perhaps the organization is attempting to launch a program that you have already seen fail at another location. Maybe you perceive the budget to be too small, the project goals too diverse or the staffing insufficient to the operational demands.

Recommendations should be offered sparingly. Your primary reason for undertaking a site visit is to learn, not teach. Help out when you can, but do not complicate your role by becoming everybody's dependable purveyor of unsolicited advice. (More on this matter later.)

Your Homework Assignment

Before you visit an organization, or ask its representatives to visit you at your office, you have some homework to complete. Successful meetings demand preparation. A site visit or interview with grantseekers is not a chance encounter; it is a planned, purposeful tool for communicating vital information. "Winging it" is a profound disservice to everybody involved and a sign of arrogance on your part.

Prior to leaving your office, make certain you have completed the following tasks:

- **Read the proposal carefully** and analyze its strengths and weaknesses, noting the key points you want to cover during your visit.

  Keep in mind that the people you are meeting will assume your fluency with their proposal. Why else would you be visiting them? If you show up to the meeting as a blank slate, hoping to absorb all pertinent information on the spot, you are almost certain to miss central issues, confuse the staff with your unapologetic ignorance and convey the corrosive message that your foundation does not really take its philanthropic role very seriously.

  Even if you have carefully read the proposal several weeks earlier, took good notes and feel confident about your comprehension, read it again just before your visit. Few people can contain myriad prospective projects in their working memories without confusing the details. Keep your acquaintance with the proposal fresh.

- **Write down the questions** you want to ask. Do not imagine that you will remember them all; nobody does. What is more, the process of formulating your list will jog your mind in useful ways, suggesting related issues that you might have otherwise overlooked. It will also remind you of what you already know and, therefore, need not bother to explore during your limited allotted time. Finally, your list will convey the proper note of seriousness: You have prepared for your visit and expect that the organization has done the same.

- **Learn enough about the field** so that you can participate intelligently in the conversation. If you are going to visit a child care center, but you have never been to one before, you know nothing about the field, and you could not tell a national model from a felonious mess, then you are probably not going to be a very effective observer. In such occasions, you need to undertake some remedial education: read articles and books, talk to the experts and colleagues, make unofficial visits to similar sites. One of the great privileges of working as a foundation executive or program officer is the opportunity to continue your education about the issues and institutions that matter most in our society. One of the job's prime responsibilities is making certain your ignorance, however forgivable, remains temporary and no worthwhile organization is made to suffer because of a lazy learning curve.

- **Only now call the organization to set up your appointment** for a mutually convenient day and hour. If the managers need time to tidy up their offices and reconfigure their plans, respond accordingly. You want the visit to be as productive as possible; catching people unaware should not be part of the agenda.

Be sure to tell the organization's director how long you will want to visit. Two hours seems typical for the first visit; in some circumstances, an entire day may be justified. Budget sufficient time to cover all your questions and allow enough flexibility so that if something interesting develops, you can roll with it.

Tell the executive director exactly what you hope to learn. (This should be easy because you have already studied the proposal and composed a list of questions.) When you are done, ask if there are other points, places or people that you should also discuss, visit or meet.

Finally, stipulate precisely who you would like to meet. Inevitably, you will want to talk with the executive director, the project manager, and perhaps a board member. In some instances, you may want to meet the organization's clients or constituents, particularly if you have questions about the project's ability to serve them effectively. If so, meeting with them separately may be more appropriate.

Keep in mind, however, that most clients know little about organizational philosophy, management, operations or finances. They simply do not ponder these matters with the same degree of interest or motivation as the staff. If they are being served—even at a minimal level—they may express their complete satisfaction. Conversely, if they are not getting what they imagine to be their due, they could lapse into uninformed ire. In most cases, however, you can count on people's sense of courtesy preventing them from complaining in front of the agency staff.

- **Dig a little deeper** for other informed perspectives. The site visit should not be the only informational expedition you undertake. Before you leave your office, you might also talk with the organization's colleagues, collaborators and competitors. You could discuss their performance with other funders or government agencies. Just keep in mind that you are calling up in order to listen, not offer your own opinions. Indeed, you could easily stir up a poisonous situation—not to say, a libelous one—if you are perceived to be spreading bad news about an organization, whether you have met them or not. All conversations must remain confidential.

Due Diligence

How does a foundation justify the expenditure of dollars on staff salaries and expenses? The answer is summed up in two words: due diligence.

Due diligence is the essence of what we do as program staff at a foundation. It is a term borrowed from the world of finance and connotes the synthesis of research gathered from multiple sources to guide investment decisions. Just as a savvy investor looks at more than the "bottom line" to inform his or her decisions, our definition is broader than a cost/benefit calculation. There is room for caring in the equation, but that does not mean that we accept claims of need or program effectiveness at face value.

In the best sense, due diligence is a "street smart" approach to philanthropy. We seek to penetrate the apparent/presented reality (as reflected in the proposal) to get at the backstage reality of the situation. Oftentimes things are as they appear. Most organizations are operating out of a position of integrity and cynicism is not warranted. But neither is uncritical acceptance the most appropriate stance.

How do we get to the truth? First, you have to be open to the truth, even if it is discrepant with your initial impressions or biases. It can require "listening with the third ear" to capture offhand comments or nonverbal cues that signal there is more to know. But if you make it clear by your behavior that your mind is made up or that you think you know better, no one will even send those subtle cues your way.

Due diligence is more an attitude and orientation to the work than it is a "technology" that can be summed up in a checklist. History is always relevant. In fact, the wellspring of due diligence is your connectedness to the field(s) in which you are doing your grantmaking. As you learn more of the relevant history of a field or a region, you can ask more astute questions and offer informed observations of your own, connecting you more deeply with your source. By communicating subtly that you understand the experience and point of view of the speaker, you engender trust. Networking is another essential aspect of the work. It is the solicitation and collation of multiple opinions and points of view that makes for true due diligence. It is also essential to keep up with what other funders are doing and with research, literature and policy developments in the field.

Tom David, Executive Vice President
The California Wellness Foundation

Staging the Site Visit

Site visits tend to put everybody on edge, at least initially. If you are new to the role of program officer, you will probably feel somewhat self-conscious yourself. (Who am I to judge these hard-working groups? What if I say something foolish? How will I measure up to the more seasoned program officers who have visited in the past?) Self-doubt and uncertainty is natural. In fact, every meeting should probably contain a small spark of nervousness, if only to ignite your efforts. The point is to manage the edginess on both sides so that your communication remains unclouded and you can proceed through the agenda.

Trust is an essential element in enduring human relationships, and violating it disrupts not only social relations but those between the parties in philanthropy as well. Foundation officers need to remember that applicants are personally involved in their proposals and convinced, rightly or wrongly, that their projects are important, original and worth funding. Treating grantseekers rudely or arrogantly is inexcusable. Foundations should acknowledge that applicants are essential and should establish a code of conduct with them based on honesty and respect. Honesty is asking questions about projects directly, being clear about how proposals are reviewed, and making evaluations that are forthright, not vague or evasive. Honesty is telling applicants up front that proposals do not have much chance to be funded and giving a clearer idea why proposals were rejected. Respect is approaching grantseekers as partners, not as supplicants who must come on bended knee. Respect is responding to them promptly and making an effort to describe the rationale used in grant decisions, even it if subjects foundation logic to scrutiny by those not truly qualified to judge.

McIlnay, Dennis P. *How Foundations Work: What Grantseekers Need to Know About the Many Faces of Foundations*, Jossey-Bass Publishers, 1998.

Over time, interviews and site visits will begin to feel comfortable as you make more and more of them.

If you are not completely at ease right now, imagine how the applicant feels. A site visit multiplies hopes. You have indicated interest in the organization's grant proposal. Eventually, your visit will lead to a recommendation: either to disburse or to deny funds. Some organizations will have difficulty shaking this fact from their mind: Money will be the persistent subtext of their experience with you. That is an unflattering prospect, but true nonetheless. Only the most experienced nonprofit managers will perceive that you can help them in other ways, such as rethinking their program strategies or forging links to other service providers.

In the worst cases, this can lead to an adversarial standoff. The organization wants their grant and you are searching for reasons not to give it to them.

This undercuts and undervalues the relationship between your foundation and the applicant. You should not be conducting a site visit for the purpose of mounting criticism or withholding support. You are not aiming to be an obstacle. Rather, you should always be searching for potentially powerful collaborators with whom you can help ameliorate some of the world's problems and magnify its beauty. Your foundation's wealth is truly valuable only when it can be placed at the disposal of effective organizations.

Location, Location, Location

Consider the basics of conversational comfort. If you are conducting an interview at the organization's site, make certain you have secured a quiet, private location. If the executive director insists on occupying a busy spot full of jangling telephones and incessant foot traffic, ask to relocate. Assure him or her you want to devote your full attention to the interview and, by implication, you expect the same.

If the interview is scheduled for your office, be aware of your foundation's various and often unconscious declarations of institutional wealth and power. Even if you do not occupy a fancy office, subtle reminders of the disparity between the grantgiver and grantseeker may intimidate, distract or even provoke your visitors.

Be assured that you cannot make this disparity disappear. But you can reduce it to a tolerable level. Remember to

- shake off the initial stiffness by shaking hands and offering a warm, congenial smile.
- step out from behind your desk to meet your guests.
- set up the seats to suggest collegial exchange.
- offer coffee, tea, juice, water, perhaps something to snack on.
- smile again, relax and enjoy your encounter because if you are not comfortable, the other person is really going to squirm.
- most important: be prepared to listen.

Staying on Track

A good grantmaker manages the meeting. To accomplish this task, you must stay on top of three factors.

- **Time**. Keep everybody apprised of your time limitations from the outset. If you have scheduled a two-hour visit, gently remind the applicant of your schedule. Clear time constraints help everybody maintain the proper pace so that you do not find yourself cramming two hours worth of crucial talk and observation into the last 20 minutes.

- **Goals**. Review your agenda with the people in charge: These are the five things I would like to accomplish during this visit. One, I want to walk around your site and take a look at your operations. Two, I would like to meet several of the frontline staff. Three, I want to talk with your executive director about finances. Four, I would like to have a conversation about your plans for the future with your board members. And five, I want to be certain to leave enough time for you to talk with me about anything on your mind. Finally, I want to answer any questions you may have about how our foundation operates.

- **Focus**. To profit from your visit, you need to free your mind of extraneous matters. If you are thinking about lunch, your next interview or all the work left moldering back on your desk at the foundation office, then you might as well not be at the site visit. In fact, only by assuming an engaged, energetic listening manner—the kind of attentiveness that wears you out by the end of the day—will you be able to keep the conversation on-track when it threatens to stray. Of course, it is easy enough to talk about the necessity of keeping one's mind clear; it is considerably more difficult to do so.

Site Visit Sample Agenda

I.   Introduction

II. Review the agenda; establish time lines

III. Tour the facilities

IV. Brief presentation of proposal by grantseekers

V.   Discussion; questions and answers

VI. The review and approval process

VII. Timing/next steps

Chapter 3: Conducting Site Visits and Interviews

Paying attention is one of the skills that you will cultivate over time as a program officer: the result of practice, heightened confidence and self-discipline.

How Do You Know When a Site Visit is Going Badly?

The site visit comes in all shapes, shades and sizes. For new program officers in particular, it can be difficult to tell when a visit is going well because success also assumes many forms.

However, it is rather easy to recognize when the site visit is falling apart and threatening to leave you with nothing to show for your effort. Among the tell-tale signs:

- **Nobody knows the answers** to your questions. What does this indicate? Perhaps the group is hiding something, or maybe they really do not know the answers. Indeed, perhaps nobody has ever posed your questions before. Or your questions are too vague, complex or irrelevant to elicit an intelligent response—another entirely plausible explanation.

- **Key people fail to show up** for your visit, despite clear and repeated requests. Among the more troubling absences: the bookkeeper or chief financial officer, board members, the project manager or the executive director. Without the people who can address your questions, the visit is pointless.

- **You have a bad feeling** about the organization in general. Does something look, sound or feel wrong? Are you confused about what is actually happening on an operational basis? Does the real action seem to be somewhere else? Are you thankful you are not a client using this agency? Sometimes you have to trust your instincts and then ask yourself: What is the matter here?

Site Visits by Wandering Around

In some cases, you will need to flesh out your conversation with the executive director and board members by actually watching the organization in action. Indeed, if feasible, it is almost always worth the effort. By spending an hour or so with the frontline staff and perhaps some of their clients, you will glimpse a portion of the organizational reality that usually eludes the formal interview process. On the most basic level, you will want to find out if the group is doing what it claims: Does the child care center provide a warm, safe, clean environment for its kids? Do the clinic workers deliver a steady stream of health services to the poor? Is the arts organization offering music lessons and staging concerts?

Beyond your (admittedly) cursory inspection, you will have a chance to talk with the people delivering services. Ask them what makes their work worthwhile? How do they measure progress? What impedes their efforts? Why have they dedicated their professional lives to this particular field and this organization?

In many groups, the division between the administration and the service-delivery staff proves considerable. That is not necessarily a problem. It does mean that if you spend all your time in the administrative offices, you will only end up with part of the picture.

Meetings with People You Just Plain Do Not Like

Occasionally, you will find yourself meeting with a staff or board member who rubs you the wrong way. It is inevitable; even the most open-minded person cannot take a shine to everybody. Like most of life's uncomfortable moments, this situation presents both dangers and opportunities.

To avoid consigning an unpleasant person to the trash heap of your affections and thus unfairly scuttling his organization's chances for support, you must ask yourself: Why, exactly, do I feel put off? Is it because I am reminded of my overbearing brother, selfish sister-in-law, the neighbor who never cleans up his yard? If so, the demons of ill will are pretty easy to wave away. Recognize your part in the unfortunate encounter, be more accommodating than your inclinations urge and get on with your interview.

On the other hand, if this person's hubris, hectoring or humorlessness appears to interfere with his managerial duties, then you may have stumbled into a more complicated dilemma. Obnoxious individuals seldom make good managers. When faced with an unusually difficult person at the head of a strong organization with sound plans and a good reputation, you will need to peer more deeply into the organizational dynamics to see if some kind of personnel disaster is brewing off-stage. Indeed, it is crucial in these situations to acknowledge your feelings so that they will lead to a fair and thorough investigation.

Excavating Information

Once you have arrived for your site visit, what should you be looking for? Most simply, you can focus your quest on five essential issues:

- What is really happening?
- How is it happening?
- Who is involved?
- What does the physical appearance of the site indicate?
- What is the public benefit derived from the effort?

Visiting the Board

The board remains the key to institutional stability, program vision and the oversight of any grant you might eventually award. That is why you may wish to talk with a board representative. If the board is operating properly, you can discuss its vision and philosophy; if the board is not certain about its mission and goals, that is also worth knowing.

However, you should also be careful that your visit does not inadvertently drive a wedge between the staff and board. Do not caucus privately with board members unless you have an exceptionally good reason. If, for example, the organization finds itself in the throes of a difficult leadership transition, you may have no other choice than to work almost exclusively with the board. If the board urgently requests a private meeting, you should probably honor their feelings while making certain that your presence does not contribute to strife between the organization's governing body and its employees. If you have concerns about the organization's management, you may need to speak in confidence with key board members.

Producing the information that can answer these questions is, unsurprisingly, a complicated task. To this end, you will need to rely on a mixture of direct observation and conversation seasoned with strategic curiosity.

Of course, it is also worth noting at this point that you will run into agencies that simply are very well-run. You will not need to strenuously inspect the situation; you will not have to head off to the interview worried about what you may find. Instead, you will quickly recognize that the proposal is sensible, the agency is well-managed, its reputation appears solid, the results of its efforts are self-evident. In these cases, there really is not anything to dig up. Your mission is to build rapport and construct a basis for your long-term collaboration—a happy duty.

ASKING THE RIGHT (AND WRONG) QUESTIONS

Many site visits, however, will demand more thoughtful inquiry. Although one cannot specify the precise questions that you should habitually ask, it is possible to suggest the qualities that will best serve your inquiry.

- **Variety.** Throughout your visit, ask different kinds of questions. Mix the specific ("How many clients will you serve next year?") with the open-ended ("Tell me about your development campaign."), as well as the unabashedly reflective ("What moments in your work have told you that you are on the right course?").

- **Order.** Ask questions in a logical progression. If you have five questions about staffing, work through them consecutively. If you jump around, you will confuse everybody and add an unwanted dash of chaos to an already complex encounter.

- **Permission.** Sometimes you will need to coax out details about the less pleasant aspects of organizational life. For instance, if you suspect that the board has been battling recently with staff, then a general question—"How are your board and staff relations?"—may not suffice. You will almost inevitably hear, "Oh, they are pretty good." Better to say: "Lots of organizations experience stress between their staff and board; it is really in the nature of the nonprofit structure. What are the points of conflict in your organization?" In this way, you have made their problem universal, relieved the pressure and given them the opportunity to be honest with you without fearing that you will misunderstand.

- **Good faith.** Formulate genuine questions whose answers will illuminate your understanding of the organization and its mission. Avoid any hint of sarcasm, meanness or self-righteous pique. Do not set traps. A grantmaker is neither a private investigator nor a public prosecutor.

THE ALL-IMPORTANT LAST QUESTIONS

Toward the conclusion of your interview, do not forget to ask the following:

- What should I know that I have not asked you?
- What are you worried that I might have misunderstood?
- Is there anything that we have left out?

These questions go straight to the heart of your task: informing yourself about the organization in the most thorough and pertinent way possible. It also reinforces another essential truth: You are not the expert; they are. You are there to learn from them.

Ten Interviewing Styles to Avoid at All Costs

Perhaps it is easier to categorically state how you should not behave as an interviewer. In all situations, avoid the temptation to be a

1. **Big talker.** You love the sound of your own voice. You know that you have great wisdom to impart and act on this conviction without restraint. You are happy to endlessly relate your own theories, opinions and exploits, while the interview subject provides scant detail, parrots your prejudices and shies away from offering his or her own views.

2. **Agile anticipator.** You affect an Olympian omniscience. You know the answers before they are given. At end the interview, you leave with a mixture of erroneous ideas, foggy recollections and half-truths.

3. **Listless listener.** You are bored. You have heard all these answers many times before. You find yourself thinking about lunch or mulling over what your next question will be before you hear the answer to the present one.

4. **Prosecuting attorney.** You proceed as if cross-examining a hostile witness. You put the interviewee on guard, grill him or her remorselessly and suppress the open expression of differing ideas.

5. **Goodwill ambassador.** You have an aversion to asking difficult or sensitive questions. You skirt around the prospect of unpleasantness. You abhor offending people; you want to make friends.

6. **Captious categorizer.** You are blessed with second sight, able to intuitively judge people's hidden motives. You classify others according to your own biases. You are the proud victim of your own prejudices.

7. **Simultaneous doer.** During interviews held at your foundation, you perform like a one-person office: answering telephone calls, signing letters, dispatching duties to your staff. You are just too busy to give the interview your full attention.

8. **Faulty question framer.** You ask leading questions, telegraphing the answers you desire to hear. You ask general questions that produce general answers. You dabble in vague and incoherent inquiries and then interrupt with new, equally confusing questions before you get your answers.

9. **Triple-header questioner.** You compose ridiculously complex questions with multiple parts that prove difficult to answer and impossible to track. A typical example: "Tell me all about your programs and how you raise money for them and then conduct their evaluation."

10. **Tactless tactician.** You hone in on personal questions, such as salary concerns, in front of other staff. You phrase your inquiries in a crude, rude and tasteless manner. It has never occurred to you that people might be offended.

Avoiding Evasions

Some people prove rather artful at not answering questions. Consider the story of one site visit recounted by a foundation colleague.

The program officer had rendezvoused with the executive director at the construction site of the organization's new offices. For the next two hours, they toured the site, speaking with the contractor, the architect, some of the crew. The pair never stopped walking; they never sat down to rest. No time was allotted to exchange information, engage in conversation or even take a few notes. The director was charming, funny and full of energy; but she avoided answering all questions about finances. At the end of the tour, the director gushed over the wonderful opportunity to meet the program officer, shook hands goodbye and disappeared into the mist. The whole visit had been exquisitely orchestrated and it proved entirely unsatisfying. The program officer had observed the hole in the ground destined to be the new facility, but she did not learn a thing about the organization's programs and capacity, its sources for additional funding, its current budget, its vision for the future. The program officer had been handled—and by experts, it seemed.

How can you avoid this kind of situation? First, as we discussed earlier, you must do your homework. Given a clear sense of purpose, a roster of pertinent questions and a timely schedule, you will find yourself justifiably intolerant of distractions and determined to reach the heart of the matter with due diligence. When your hosts do veer off toward the elusive and the extraneous, you will be better prepared to rein them back in.

Sometimes, you will just have to put your foot down. If the executive director wants to show you something off-site, make certain this unexpected "opportunity" does not obstruct your primary purpose. Remind the people in charge about the five things you must learn within the limits of your two-hour visit.

Nevertheless, if an organization is determined to evade your questions, you cannot squeeze information out of them. In these cases, you may need to compose a list of all the questions left unanswered during your site visit when you return to your office and then immediately send a letter to the board and staff with a request that the additional information to be supplied in writing.

What do you do when you are confronted with an outright lie? First, you must consider the source. Is the speaker compensating for a lack of knowledge? Repeating a half-truth that has achieved full currency inside the organization over time? Attempting to protect someone else? Acting on orders? ("Whatever she asks you, do not tell her about this year's budget shortfall.") Lapsing into habitual exaggeration? Omitting the unflattering? Are they simply, boldly, misstating the truth?

In any case, you will probably need to confront the prevaricator. Given the perils of libel, the psychology of denial and the discomfort you are likely to experience, it is best to proceed diplomatically. ("Your answer surprises me. I have always understood the situation differently. Could you explain further?" or, "Am I misinformed? Why do I have the impression that the situation is really more complicated?")

The Art of Observation

Beyond asking questions, you will also want to keep your eyes open. What are you looking for? You should pay attention to both the concrete and the intangible.

Let us say you are visiting a community clinic. You will naturally want to see if it is actually providing the medical services that its managers assert. But you should also be noticing other things. Are an ample number of people using its services? Making appointments? Benefiting from its existence? Is the staff pleasant, busy, cooperative, committed? What do the examination rooms look like? What do the decor, lighting and acoustics convey? What does the site tell you about the organization's self-image and its attitude toward the clients?

When you are roaming through the administrative offices, you might cull insights from something as (apparently) inconsequential as the telephones. Are they ringing all the time or does the site resound with eerie, disheartening silence?

If you are visiting an organization with multiple sites—for example, a healthcare agency with five different clinics—then you must cope with the inevitability that you will be escorted to the very best one. Insist on seeing something "different"—the clinic located at the other end of town, the site with the newest staff, the operation that is still "in development." Again, you are not aiming to ensnare or embarrass your hosts. Rather, you are in pursuit of a fully-rounded organizational portrait.

A Final Word about Advice

It is always tricky giving advice. But as noted earlier, there are occasions when it is important to do so, as long as two conditions prevail.

■ You have information, perspective, experience or a word of caution that may truly benefit the organization.

■ The people with power inside the organization are prepared to listen, consider and use your advice.

Even when advice is crucial, it must be delivered with grace and sensitivity. Make certain your words are understood to be an offering that can be declined.

The language you use will highlight your intentions. If you speak in terms roughly the equivalent of "Now let me tell you how to do it," then the organization will understandably interpret your advice as a directive. Instead, you might approach the matter with tactical diffidence: "I have seen organizations take a variety of approaches in a situation like yours…" You could simply respond to their explication of a particular problem by asking them to puzzle it out for themselves. ("Yes, that is an interesting problem. What do you think is going on? What would you need to resolve this situation?") Sometimes, the best assistance you can give is to assume a Socratic role, persistently asking the organization to define its own terms of success, while echoing back a critically attuned version of what you have just heard.

You must also be aware that some groups will request your advice when they do not really want it. They are flattering you, hoping you will feel part of their organization. Still others will confuse your questions with advice. You ask, "Have you thought about merging with a like-minded organization in town?" They hear, "If you want our money, you better merge." On these occasions, it is crucial to assure the organization that sometimes a question really is just a question. ("Yes, I am actually wondering: Does a merger make sense? I do not know. You are the expert; tell me what you think.")

Be aware that when you do offer advice, sound or otherwise, most organizations will feel compelled to regard it very seriously. This is particularly true for small and mid-sized organizations. (When a large institution, such as a university, confronts bad advice from a program officer, its director can usually smile agreeably, pretend to take notes while actually doodling and then shake your hand goodbye, wondering why the foundation hired somebody like you.) Smaller, poorer, less experienced groups are more vulnerable. They will feel that you have just made them an offer they cannot refuse, even if it is a terrible one. It takes real strength of character to say, "Well, thanks, but no thanks. That may be good advice for some groups, but it is not really something we are interested in." Do not put anybody in this bind.

An Eye on Results

Finally, you can keep your site visit on track by recalling a simple, yet often elusive truth about the proper relationship between foundations and nonprofits: It is not about you. It is not about them. Your chief concern should always be focused on the people you are both aiming to serve.

Ultimately, your attention should be directed toward poor children, working families, participants in the arts and culture, the sick and the dying, students, advocates for ecosystems and animals—whatever your foundation's focus may be.

Of course, you hope to establish fruitful, perhaps even long-term relationships with the organizations seeking your support. Naturally, you want your personal relations to be cordial, honest, stimulating, gratifying. But most of all—and this cannot be overemphasized—you want to be certain that your foundation's money is going to be used in the most productive way possible. To accomplish this goal, you must step forward to serve as a broker between potential partners with their proper collaboration resulting in greater numbers of people living full, just, healthy, happy and productive lives.

Ending Well

How do you know when you are done with the site visit or interview? Simply put, it is time to leave when you have learned enough; but how much is enough?

An enterprising grantmaker can always dig up something new during the course of a prolonged visit, treating him- or herself to the unpredictable alarms and diversions of organizational life. But that is not your proper role. Rather, you should concentrate on acquiring enough knowledge so that you can return to your office and make an intelligent, informed recommendation about funding.

The appropriate moment for departure is often signaled by the fact that you have

- received credible answers to your questions,
- acquired a "feel" for the organization's staff, board and site,
- reached a point of consistency, where the people you are talking with reiterate the same basic information,
- exhausted your own curiosity about the key issues raised by the organization's proposal.

Saying Goodbye

When you recognize that it will soon be time to conclude your visit, you should indicate your readiness to the executive director and board. Then take a moment to summarize what you have discussed together and what you have observed on your own. Remind the staff of any questions left hanging that may require follow-up. Note the items that demand preparation, such as financial statements, position papers, board membership lists or insurance certifications. Do not forget to ask the agency staff if they have any questions. The site visit is as much an opportunity for the grantseeker to learn about your institution as for you to learn about theirs.

Finally, explain your foundation's decisionmaking process to the applicant. Rest assured: Nothing matters more to the organization than these next several steps. Their eyes, always, are on your foundation's actions leading to the approval or rejection of their grant. Therefore, in all fairness, the organization's staff and board should be apprised of

- your foundation's method for reviewing and approving grants,
- the role your foundation's staff and board will play respectively in this process,
- the timeline for notifying the organization of your decision,
- the rough odds of getting a grant (which might be indicated by noting the number of proposals you receive and the percentage of grants approved).

Organizations may also benefit from a review of your foundation's aims and philosophy. Summarize the kinds of grants you have awarded in the past, your current priorities, your plans for the future. If your annual report fairly reflects your present operations, leave a copy with the organization. The point is not to trumpet your sound policies and past recommendations. Rather, you are striving to demystify your foundation's approach to philanthropy and thereby minimize the organization's understandable anxiety about the future.

A word of caution: Do not make any commitments about the disposition of their grant. Such promises are entirely inappropriate. Even if you feel wildly enthusiastic—or profoundly negative—you should not disclose your intended recommendation; that is overstepping your role. Indeed, one of the worst things that a program officer can do during a site visit is mislead an organization into believing that the decision has already been made. In the end, your foundation's board will approve or reject the organization's proposal. You are a crucial part of the decisionmaking process; but you are rarely the final arbiter. To suggest otherwise is dishonest, irresponsible and even cruel.

After You Leave

Once the site visit has concluded, you have one final task: You must take the time to debrief yourself. It is best to formalize this process. Schedule 20 or 30 uninterrupted minutes at your desk to recollect your experience and make sense of your ideas, hunches, sensations and hesitations. Take notes. Ask yourself

- What did I want to learn from the site visit?
- What did I learn?

- What do I still need to understand about the organization in order to make a sound decision about their grant request?
- After you have finished reviewing the organization, take a few more minutes to evaluate your own performance. Ask yourself
- If I were going to conduct the site visit over again tomorrow, what would I do differently?
- What new questions would I ask?
- What other places might I want to inspect; what other people should I meet?
- Did my actions today facilitate or impede the flow of information?
- Did I say anything that I now wish I had not?
- Did I leave out any important information?

If you are honest with yourself, you will probably conclude that your performance during the site visit rated something less than perfect. This imperfection is a sure sign that you are, like the rest of us, human. Do not berate yourself for mistakes or oversights; learn from them. Make a commitment to draw upon your experience and improve your skills over time. This advice pertains not merely to your first few months on the job, but for the duration of your career.

Grantmakers do not master their craft in weeks or even months. Your knowledge and abilities should continue to expand over the years, if you conscientiously seek their improvement.

Indeed, your continuing professional development should become an abiding personal priority. You owe it to yourself and your foundation. Most of all, you owe it to the countless nonprofit organizations who will come to rely on your judgement, integrity and skills far into the future.

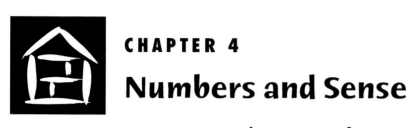

CHAPTER 4
Numbers and Sense

Learning to Look at Nonprofit Finances

Let us begin with some heresy.
You do not need accounting skills, calculus or a background on Wall Street to evaluate the state of a nonprofit organization's finances. It is not nearly that difficult.

In terms of technical expertise, you will merely need to exercise your basic math skills—simple addition, subtraction, multiplication, division—although, you might want to bring along your calculator.

That does not mean that financial analysis is not important. It is just that the real challenges, as we shall see, reside in realms other than the mathematical. In the end, the review of your grantees' finances calls for many of the same skills and attitudes that you apply to proposal reading and site visits. Ideally, the numbers will align themselves with the narrative; they will speak to the same points.

Your task, once again, is to learn how to listen and, as important, ask the right questions.

Math Phobics among Us

If the prospect of reviewing an applicant's finances causes you to vibrate with anxiety, you can take some comfort in the fact that you are not alone. Many grantmaking professionals are prone to math phobia.

Given the background of most foundation program officers, this fear seems almost inevitable. Foundation professionals are often recruited from the program side of the nonprofit sector; almost never from the financial offices. Look at your peers. Among them you will find professional grantmakers who formerly served as executive directors, program administrators, social workers, educators, evaluators, consultants, but rarely a former controller, bookkeeper or financial manager.

The standard division between the foundation world's program people and financial staff does not help matters, either. Large foundations usually hire very talented and experienced professionals to oversee their own finances. But program staff rarely confer with them when assessing the fiscal health of a grant applicant. In small foundations, financial record keeping is frequently passed to outside accountants, diminishing opportunities for obtaining in-house advice from the more mathematically inclined.

Given this background and professional environment, why would you feel confident about diving into a sea of numbers?

The Oddities of Nonprofit Finance

The financial peculiarities of the nonprofit sector also complicate matters.

Remember: Nonprofits are not simply for-profit ventures run at a loss. They are built upon a different set of financial assumptions, some of which may appear perplexing and even perverse to individuals accustomed to the private sector, such as your board members. To begin, nonprofits often depend on volunteers, a resource whose value eludes accurate accounting on the balance sheet. Nonprofits rely on varied and shifting funding sources, usually a volatile mix of earned income and contributions. In the nonprofit world, financial security is almost always perceived as a major challenge, if not an impossibility.

With these qualities, you might think that an extremely complex and sophisticated set of accounting procedures would be required to chart nonprofit enterprise. Just the opposite is true.

Some grantmakers look at a financial statement first to give them a sense of the scale of the operations, the stability of the organization and the balance among income streams. But no foundation officer has ever proclaimed "I wasn't really impressed by their project, but the financial accounting looked so good that I decided to recommend the grant anyway."

Reasonable Goals for Financial Reporting

What can you hope to learn from a grant applicant's financial information? In truth, there are only a handful of fundamental issues to consider. Almost always, you will need to ask the following:

- Have the organization's finances been residing in the black for an appropriate period of time? (Are they breaking even or even making money?)
- When was the last time the organization dipped into the red? (Are they losing money and how much for how long?)
- Do their debts exceed their available cash? (Do organizational finances look like they are about to crash?)
- Have they budgeted enough money for the proposed project? (Or conversely, are they padding the budget to cover unrelated expenses?)
- Is there something unusual here that is worth discussing (e.g., loans from board members, a liability in the books for unpaid salaries, a large amount of short-term debt with assets tied up in buildings and equipment)?

Questions along these lines always weigh heavy in the grantmaker's mind because they speak to our three greatest, if characteristically unuttered fears:

1. Awarding a grant to an organization that promptly goes bankrupt.

2. Supporting a group that subsequently gains public attention through embezzlement, misappropriation of funds or some other financial scandal.

3. Making a grant when the organization does not really need the funds.

Note that fear of failure in a program area is generally not regarded as an embarrassment commensurate with financial failure. Perhaps that is because experience makes grantmakers more realistic about the fate of programmatic aspirations; we understand that some degree of failure is routine, even inevitable. (It might be even argued that if every project you support qualifies as an unalloyed success, then you are not taking enough risks in your grantmaking.) Financial failure may also carry a more pointed psychological weight because of its bald obviousness and disrepute. (Impending bankruptcy or financial scandal can be accompanied by very embarrassing publicity.) On the other hand, failure in nonprofit programming is neither rarely concrete nor easily quantifiable.

Of course, no responsible grantmaker wants to recommend a grant to an organization inclined toward waste or larceny. But this entirely justifiable expectation of fiscal competency, reliability and honesty also prompts funders to overload their grantees with financial reporting requirements. Resist this temptation.

Today many nonprofits support a huge burden of mandated financial reports whose benefit to both the funder and the organization are dubious. Do not needlessly add to this burden. Keep your requirements sleek and practical. To put it another way: Do not allow the paper reports to clog your real opportunity for understanding.

What is this opportunity? Frank, far-ranging and continuous conversation about finances.

Talking about More Than Numbers
CONVERSATION AS THE KEY TO UNDERSTANDING FINANCES

Most grantmakers ask surprisingly few questions about finances.

They may speak for hours with applicants about program goals and strategies; they can offer penetrating queries on staffing and evaluation. But when the subject turns to finances, most of us too often remain mute.

Perhaps it is the fear factor, the unsettling sense that financial analysis is not really our realm. Perhaps we are embarrassed to ask for clarifications when we suspect that the answers may lie right under our noses, glaring up in the black-and-white of confounding enumeration. Maybe it is because many grantseekers and grantmakers are equally uncomfortable when it comes to talking finances. We jointly construct a conspiracy of silence.

Whatever the reasons, it undermines our ability to comprehend the genuine state of nonprofit enterprise and makes our relationships with grantseekers much murkier than need be. But this difficulty should not surprise anybody.

Honest disclosure about money is hard even among friends and family. (Can we expect that much more from funders and grantees?) The trick here is to acknowledge the difficulty and then move on. Frank discussion should be a mark of respect, a signal that you are willing to share a moment of existential uncertainty, the give-and-take of problem solving. You discuss finances so that you may understand one another on the most fundamental level.

What kinds of issues should your conversation surround? For starters, you can learn a great deal about nonprofits by sitting down with the executive director, and perhaps a board member, and steer the discussion toward the following general topics:

1. How do you assess your current financial situation?
2. What are you worried about with regard to your finances?
3. How do your financial concerns affect daily decisionmaking?
4. What items in your budget or financial reports do you want to draw my attention to?
5. What happens when the hoped-for grant runs out?

Gazing at records and reports alone in your office will not answer these questions. You must engage the nonprofit staff in honest, but amiable conversation to learn

- where the organization is going, given its current financial state,
- what stands in the way of the organization reaching its goals,
- how you as a grantmaker can most powerfully assist the organization in achieving its objectives, attaining stability, maximizing its impact and extending its reach.

The mere fact that you raise these kinds of questions can significantly alter the thinking, perhaps even the behavior, of your nonprofit partners. When you wonder aloud why the executive director's salary is so low, how the reserve fund will be accumulated or where the following year's funding might come from, then you may be elevating to consciousness matters that have lurked just below the organizational surface for years.

Of course, you will also meet resistance in some quarters. Nonprofit managers understand that most funders do not want to hear about their financial anxieties. With good reason, they believe that funders prefer to be reassured that their grant money will not be wasted. Nonprofits worry that their worries will only make you worry more.

Strive to meet these reasonable fears head-on. Demonstrate by the example of your open, curious questioning that you aspire to understand, not to badger, interrogate or indict the applicant.

Acknowledge your own fears about finances. State boldly, I really do not know much about this area; please educate me.

The Six Kinds of Financial Reports Commonly Submitted with Grant Proposals

Document	What You Can Learn
1. Project budget	■ What is the organization trying to do? ■ How will the project be structured, staffed and managed? ■ Based on what you know about similar projects, do the expenses seem reasonable? ■ Are the plans for income realistic? ■ Are the expenses and income consistent with the program described in the narrative? ■ Does the budget reflect cash flows?
2. Organization-wide budget	■ How does the proposed project budget fit with the organizational budget? Is it in or out of proportion with total costs and income? ■ Does the organization as a whole have appropriate income streams and a realistic budget that adequately covers core operating costs? ■ How is the budget constructed? Does it reconcile with expected cash flows? How are temporarily restricted funds handled? ■ How does the organization monitor budget to actual?
3. Audit	■ Does the organization need an annual audit? Does it have one? ■ Has the auditor issued an "unqualified opinion" showing that the organization's financial statements are fairly presented? ■ Does the audited balance sheet indicate a sufficiently stable financial context for the project to succeed?
4. Recent financial statements	■ Is the organization able to issue timely internal financial statements? ■ Are there any areas significantly different from the organizational budget or previous financial activity? If so, what are the implications?
5. Federal Form 990	■ Has the organization filed a Federal Form 990? ■ Do you feel comfortable with the proportions of program, management and general expenses and fundraising costs?
6. Schedule A to Form 990	■ Are the salaries of top paid staff reasonable and appropriate? ■ Is the list of major contributors, if included, in line with what you otherwise know about the organization?

Your conversational outreach should not be limited to the grantseekers. In the quest to extend your understanding of financial matters and to clarify the fiscal status of grant applicants, you should also consult with your in-house experts and peers. If your foundation is large enough to employ a financial officer, seek this person's assistance in decoding financial reports and budgets. Ask questions such as "Is there anything I should notice about finances in this proposal?" and "Can you help me understand this financial statement?"

By expressing your own uncertainty, coupled with a willingness to learn, you can gradually grow into mastery of nonprofit finances—a change that will benefit everybody concerned.

Fundamental Questions about Basic Documents
HOW TO TALK ABOUT THE ESSENTIALS OF NONPROFIT FINANCES

Financial reports and records translate nonprofit plans and history into dollars. Think of them as fiscal x-rays. Below the surface of the proposal's flawless reasoning and the organization's fine, fleshy prose regarding its past accomplishments, you will encounter the real bones of the matter: the costs and income sources that either hold plans and reputations together or allow them to waffle to the floor.

Unfortunately, many nonprofit managers exhibit confusion about the financial records' role in the grantmaking process. Typically, they ask their fundraising consultants or more experienced peers the following:

- Should we write the organizational budget in a way to show us losing money, making money or breaking even?
- Should we reveal the costs of all staff involved in operating the proposed project or just the personnel we think the funder might be interested in supporting?
- Should we promise to assume the project or operational costs once the foundation grant is over?

Questions like these suggest that the applicant is constructing financial materials solely to meet the perceived needs and preferences of the funder. That is an understandable impulse; more than anything, applicants want you to fund their proposals. But by anticipating your desires, instead of crafting a careful analysis of the true financial history and actual projected costs, grantseekers lead us into treacherous terrain.

For grantmakers, problems most frequently arise in interpreting financial materials when important items (for various and often understandable reasons) are omitted. Imagine your confusion when you receive a proposal in which the following occurs:

- The applicant pens a persuasive argument to stage a new season of theatrical performances, but the budget fails to reveal a line-item expense for renting the theatre.
- The executive director is budgeted to spend half of his or her time on the project, although it is merely one of the organization's dozen ongoing activities.
- Total costs do not closely approximate the amount you have seen similar organizations use in the past.

There may be a logical defense for any of these puzzling scenarios. Perhaps the performance space is donated; the project is so complex that the executive must to devote an unusual amount of time to its launching; project costs diverge because you have unfairly compared two profoundly different situations or organizations. The only way you will understand these and similar situations in which the financial materials appear to contradict the proposal narrative is to ask questions. What kinds of questions?

That entirely depends on the documents you are reviewing. Let us take a look at each of the six main documents you might receive from a grantseeker and the questions that could logically arise.

PROJECT BUDGET

The project budget is the most important financial component of the proposal. It should show the revenue and expenses related to the project. Some project budgets only reveal expenses. If this is the case, ask what income is expected for the project, if any.

Project Budget

Revenue

Foundation A	100,000
Foundation B	75,000
Corporation C	5,000
Service fees	60,000
Total revenue	**240,000**

Expenses

Project manager, 100%	45,000
Executive Director, 10%	7,500
Service delivery staff, 100%	40,000
Service delivery staff, 100%	35,000
Administrative assistant, 50%	14,000
Benefits @ 20%	35,375
Program expenses	25,000
Indirect costs @ 15%	30,281
Total expenses	**232,156**
Net	**7,844**

Analyzing the Project Budget

QUESTIONS TO ASK YOURSELF	PROJECT BUDGET		QUESTIONS TO ASK THE APPLICANT
	Revenue		
This is your foundation. Do you feel comfortable funding this percentage of the project?	Foundation A	100,000	
	Foundation B	75,000	Has this foundation been asked yet? Have they made a commitment?
	Corporation C	5,000	Has this corporation made a commitment? What experience do you have obtaining corporate grants?
If this is a first-year project, is this a reasonable estimate?	Service fees	60,000	
Overall, does this total amount seem reasonable for the project described in the proposal narrative?	**Total revenue**	**240,000**	Approximately how many people does this number represent? How did you arrive at this estimate?

Analyzing the Project Budget

QUESTIONS TO ASK YOURSELF	PROJECT BUDGET	QUESTIONS TO ASK THE APPLICANT
	Expenses	
Do these salaries seem adequate to attract people with the qualifications described in the proposal narrative?	Project manager, 100% 45,000	Do you have someone in mind for this job? Tell me about him or her.
	Executive Director, 10% 7,500	
	Service delivery staff, 100% 40,000	Will any of these people come from current staff?
	Service delivery staff, 100% 35,000	
	Administrative assistant, 50% 14,000	Is this a half-time person or is this person "shared" with another program?
Are there line items that you expected to see but did not?	Benefits @ 20% 35,375	This percentage seems low compared with other grantees. Comments?
Does this amount seem reasonable for the scope of the project described?	Program expenses 25,000	Tell me more about these expenses. I have found that different organizations use this term to mean different things. What do you include in this item? For example, is rent included? Accounting time?
Is this number reasonable given the size of the project's overall budget?	Indirect costs @ 15% 30,281	I noticed that there was not a line item for renting space for these 3–4 new staff. Will you be needing to rent new space? If not, is their share of the rent included in the "indirect costs" line item?
Is this number reasonable given the size of the project's overall budget?	**Total expenses** **232,156**	Do you feel that this amount is reasonable for what this project will accomplish?
	Net **7,844**	Will any additional funds be used for the program in the subsequent year?
		Will your core costs be covered through other funding? What is the source of this funding?
		Where will the funding for next year come from, after this grant is over?

Chapter 4: Numbers and Sense

What Does It Mean If...

...the project budget shows a deficit? Ask the applicant. It may mean that the organization intends to use some unrestricted funds to help pay for the program's expenses. It may also mean that the organization has not finished planning for the project's viability.

...the project budget shows a big surplus? It may mean that the organization wants to raise enough money this year to carry the project part way into the next year. Or it may mean that the organization has put in wildly optimistic revenue projections so that the actual revenue will be enough to pay for the project's expenses.

ORGANIZATION WIDE BUDGET

If the organization's budget is broken out into programs, it will help you assess the following:

- Is the proposed program an appropriate size compared to the rest of the organization?
- Are the organization's priorities reflected in the level of activity allocated to the various programs?

AUDIT

An audit assesses the fairness of the financial statements. Conducted by an independent Certified Public Accountant (CPA), audits are required by the federal government only for organizations that receive $300,000 or more in federal funds during the year.[4] Some state governments have additional requirements for audits, but because many small nonprofits do not get annual audits, the lack of an audit is not necessarily an issue.

Here is an introduction to the components of an audit report:

Independent Auditor's Report	
We have audited the accompanying statements of financial position of XYZ Nonprofit Organization as of December 31, 1999, and the related statements of support, revenue and expenses and changes in fund balances, changes in financial position and functional expenses for the year then ended... We conducted our audit in accordance with generally accepted auditing standards. Those standards require... In our opinion, the financial statements referred to above present fairly, in all material aspects, the financial position of the XYZ Nonprofit Organization as of December 31, 1999, the results of its activities and changes in its financial position for the year then ended in conformity with generally accepted accounting principles.... Signed, Independent CPA	This is the cover letter. Look for the words "present fairly" to clue you that this is an "unqualified opinion"—that is, the auditor believes that, without qualifications, the financial statements that follow the opinion fairly reflects the organization's financial situation. Remember: an unqualified opinion is not a "clean bill of health" for the organization's financial status. Instead, it assures you the financial statements that follow the opinion fairly describe the organization's financial status, whether excellent or terrible.

---

[4] A special type of audit is required for organizations that spend $300,000 or more (in a given year) in total federal funds (including federal funds that have passed through state or local government agencies). This audit, performed by a CPA, is described in OMB Circular A-133 and is usually referred to as an A-133 audit.

Statement of Financial Position (formerly called the "Balance Sheet") December 31, 1999	Statement of Financial Position shows the organization's assets, liabilities and net worth at the end of its fiscal year. (Other terms for net worth are "net assets" and/or "fund balance".) The organization's basic financial strength is best identified in the Statement of Financial Position. For example, if the organization's immediate debts are larger than the organization's cash, the organization may face difficulty paying its creditors.
Statement of Activity	Formerly called the Statement of Revenue and Expense or the Income Statement.
Statement of Net Cash Flows	This is a statement only recently required for nonprofits. Despite its name, it is *not* a cash flow projection. Instead, it shows whether the cash used to pay bills came, for example, from operating income, sale of real estate or obtaining a loan. Similarly, it shows whether "extra" cash was used for operating expenses, investments, making loans or other activity.
Notes 1. Organization: The XYZ Organization is a nonprofit corporation under Section 501(c)(3) of the Internal Revenue Code... 2. Significant accounting policies:... 3. Investments consisted of the following... 4. Accounts receivable consist of the following... 5. Property and equipment consisted of the following... 6. Notes payable and lease obligations consist of the following...	The Notes are one of the most interesting parts of the audit report. Look here for confirmation of the organization's nonprofit status, more detail on some of the larger line items (such as a list of the foundations who have committed grants in the future) and information on the organization's accounting practices (such as the number of years over which equipment is depreciated).

> **Management Letter**
>
> In planning and performing our audit, we considered its internal control structure in order to determine our auditing procedures…we noted certain matters involving the internal control and its operation that we considered to be reportable conditions under standards established by the American Institute of Certified Public Accountants…
>
> The organization does not have policies and procedures in place to ensure timely identification of federal awards that are subject to the Office of Management and Budget Circular A-133 audit requirements…
>
> We recommend that the organization develop and implement a plan for performing Year 2000 compliance maintenance projects…

In some cases, the auditors will find "reportable conditions," such as a failure to reconcile cash accounts. Such points will be made in a letter to management that is a separate document from the audit report.

Even if there are no reportable conditions, auditors may choose to write such a letter commenting on, for example, the Y2K computer issue or the auditor's concern that the organization is facing bankruptcy. Management letters are not issued with every audit, and there is quite a bit of latitude about what can be addressed.

You should ask for this management letter when you request financial statements because if it is negative, it may not routinely be sent to foundations.

RECENT FINANCIAL STATEMENTS

Because audits are conducted only annually (if at all), the financial information in an audit may be many months or more than a year old. As a result, many foundations request copies of recent financial statements to give them a more up-to-date look at where the organization stands financially.

Either in the financial statements or in the audited statements, you will have the information for more detailed financial analysis.

Income and expense, compared with budget, for Year to Date (six months)

	Budget for Year to Date	Actuals Year to Date	Questions to Ask the Applicant
Revenue			
Foundation grants	100,000	40,000	Do your foundation grants typically come in the second half of the fiscal year, or does this represent some other development?
Corporate grants	15,000	60,000	What are some of the reasons you have been more successful than you had anticipated in obtaining corporate support?
Service fees	10,000	25,000	Who are some of your competitors for service fees? In what ways are you different from them?
Interest earned	6,000	4,800	How are your funds invested? Do you have an investment policy? Is there a board investments committee that oversees them?
Publication sales	80,000	40,000	What are some of your new publications? How are they distributed?
Total revenue	3,000,000	3,200,000	What are the main reasons why your revenue is higher than you had anticipated?
Expenses			
Salaries	1,450,000	1,800,000	What is the approximate number of full-time and part-time staff you have now? Salary expense seems to have gone up substantially. Is most of this due to hiring new people, or due to salary increases?
Benefits	365,000	450,000	
Rent	275,000	290,000	
Office costs	90,000	100,000	
Printing	120,000	120,000	
Equipment purchase	70,000	50,000	
Miscellaneous	150,000	160,000	This is one of the biggest line items but the term "Miscellaneous" does not tell me much. What are some of the items here, and do you feel that it works for you to have such a big catchall?
Consultants	300,000	320,000	Are these consultants who were consulting to your own organization, or were you paying people as consultants/contractors to work with your clients?
Total Expenses	2,820,000	3,200,000	

Form 990 Page by Page

Hopefully this *very* sketchy overview of Form 990 will let you see the value of this document—which applicant organizations are *already* preparing and submitting annually to the IRS. By asking for the 990, a foundation does not add any additional work for the organization, and reaps the benefits of standardized line items and forms. You can download a copy of the Form 990 at **http://ftp.fedworld.gov/pubs/irs-pdf/f990.pdf**.

On page 1 of the 990, you'll see a short version of the organization's income and expenses. A key advantage of working with the 990 is that the same line items are used by all nonprofit organizations.

For example, line 9c shows the net income or loss from special events, and line 18 shows the net income for the year.

58 GRANTMAKING BASICS: A FIELD GUIDE FOR FUNDERS

Page 2 breaks out the expenses in more detail. All expenses are classified as program services, management and general or fundraising. If the organization has been consistent in categorizing its expenses, page 2 will give you a good look at what percentage of funds are going to each of these categories.

At the bottom of page 2 is a "Statement of Program Service Accomplishments," where the organization must list activities, including the number of clients serviced, publications issued, as well as "achievements that are not measurable." This section also shows the amount of money that is spent for each activity.

Chapter 4: Numbers and Sense

Form 990 Page by Page

Page 3 has a "Balance Sheet" for the organization, for both the beginning of the year and the end of the fiscal year. For example, on line 45, you will be able to see how much cash the organization had at the beginning and the end of the year.

On lines 68–69 you can see what proportion of the organization's income is temporarily and/or permanently restricted.

60   GRANTMAKING BASICS: A FIELD GUIDE FOR FUNDERS

Because the accounting guidelines for the 990 differ in some respects from the accounting guidelines used in audits, the top part of page 4 on the 990 reconciles these differences.

The lower half of page 4 lists the board members, trustees and key employees, including their compensation.

Pay careful attention to how this question is answered and to the documents that need to be attached.

Form 990 Page by Page

> Page 5 of the 990 has a multitude of "Other Information," such as the value of in-kind (noncash) contributions on line 82b and any lobbying or political expenditures on line 85d.

Form 990 (1998)						Page **6**
Part VII Analysis of Income-Producing Activities (See Specific Instructions on page 27.)						
Enter gross amounts unless otherwise indicated.	Unrelated business income		Excluded by section 512, 513, or 514		(E) Related or exempt function income	
	(A) Business code	(B) Amount	(C) Exclusion code	(D) Amount		
93 Program service revenue:						
a						
b						
c						
d						
e						
f Medicare/Medicaid payments						
g Fees and contracts from government agencies						
94 Membership dues and assessments						
95 Interest on savings and temporary cash investments						
96 Dividends and interest from securities						
97 Net rental income or (loss) from real estate:						
a debt-financed property						
b not debt-financed property						
98 Net rental income or (loss) from personal property						
99 Other investment income						
100 Gain or (loss) from sales of assets other than inventory						
101 Net income or (loss) from special events						
102 Gross profit or (loss) from sales of inventory						
103 Other revenue: a						
b						
c						
d						
e						
104 Subtotal (add columns (B), (D), and (E))						
105 Total (add line 104, columns (B), (D), and (E))						▶
Note: (Line 105 plus line 1d, Part I, should equal the amount on line 12, Part I.)						

Part VIII Relationship of Activities to the Accomplishment of Exempt Purposes (See Specific Instructions on page 28.)

Line No. ▼ | Explain how each activity for which income is reported in column (E) of Part VII contributed importantly to the accomplishment of the organization's exempt purposes (other than by providing funds for such purposes).

Part IX Information Regarding Taxable Subsidiaries (Complete this Part if the "Yes" box on line 88 is checked.)

Name, address, and employer identification number of corporation or partnership	Percentage of ownership interest	Nature of business activities	Total income	End-of-year assets
	%			
	%			
	%			
	%			

Please Sign Here Under penalties of perjury, I declare that I have examined this return, including accompanying schedules and statements, and to the best of my knowledge and belief, it is true, correct, and complete. Declaration of preparer (other than officer) is based on all information of which preparer has any knowledge. (See General Instruction U, on page 12.)

▶ Signature of officer ▶ Date ▶ Type or print name and title.

Paid Preparer's Use Only
Preparer's signature ▶ | Date | Check if self-employed ▶ ☐ | Preparer's SSN
Firm's name (or yours if self-employed) and address ▶ | | EIN ▶ | ZIP+4 ▶

Page 6 of the 990 begins with an "analysis of income-producing activities," including income from program services, contracts with government agencies, income from rentals, etc.

Other sections on this page explain how income-producing activity is related to the organization's purpose, and gives details on any taxable subsidiaries the organization may operate.

Chapter 4: Numbers and Sense

Talking Numbers

Most of the time, your opportunities for useful talk about finances will be limited to the applicant organization's executive director. Although the director is usually the person most conversant with all aspects of the organization and its application for funding, this individual is not necessarily the resident expert on finances or the only person worth engaging in conversation.

If you choose to conduct a site visit, you may dramatically broaden your understanding of the applicant's financial status by consulting with the organization's accountant or financial officer. This person will be surprised to see you. It is an odd wrinkle in philanthropy that the person who knows the most about a particular nonprofit's finances is seldom drawn into conversation with funders. Invariably, you will benefit from this person's unique perspective and expertise. After all, you are now talking with the local expert. Let the questions fly.

Beyond inquiries tied to the basic financial documents, you might also seek out the financial officer for more general orientation. Try opening up the conversation along the following lines:

- "You know, I am not too familiar with your financial records. What should I be noticing?"
- "If you were me, what questions would you have about your finances?"
- "What do you think I am likely to overlook or misunderstand?"
- "What do funders frequently misperceive about your finances?"

When you feel that you are communicating well together and some bond of trust has been established, ask the following:

- "What worries you about your finances?"
- "Are there opportunities for fiscal growth or development that key people are overlooking?"
- "Do staff or board members need to come to grips with some unpleasant or promising aspect of financial reality that has eluded them?"

Board members can also provide insight into finances during the site visit. In addition to answering basic questions about the financial past and present, you can ask them to speculate on scenarios for the future.

- What kinds of financial problems, or opportunities, do the board see coming in the near future?
- Is there anything about the organizational finances that the board does not quite grasp?
- What kind of financial reports does the board receive, and what does it do with them?

It is a sign of health to find board members as involved with financial affairs as program matters. Indeed, their knowledge and participation may have considerable influence on your funding decision.

A Final Question

WHAT ABOUT COST EFFECTIVENESS?

One last issue remains. Is the proposed project cost-effective?

There is really no way to answer this question by consulting the documents. Budgets and financial reports seldom point to any obvious discrepancy in the organization's spending logic. Neither is cost effectiveness usually expounded upon in the proposal narrative.

Once again, you must pose the question that opens up conversation. At some point, you need to ask the following to the appropriate people:

- "Could you get equal results at less expense?"
- "Are there other ways that you might effectively structure the financing of this project?"

The answer to these questions may surprise you. You may learn that more cost-effective strategies do not work with your grantee's target population. You may learn that the program's high short-term expense actually falls far distant of the long-term price of failing to act. (Compare the costs of preventing youth violence with building and maintaining more prisons.) You may suddenly realize that you are working with a visionary start-up organization whose quest to change the world simply has not yet been leavened with the more mundane matters of cost-control. (And now you must judiciously consider whether this is the right moment to press the issue.) In short, cost-effectiveness is not everything, but it is almost always worth talking about.

Your model for financial discussions is not the Internal Revenue Service. Your aim is not to mount fault-finding, penny-pinching, miserly criticism. Instead, you simply want to know how else might good results be achieved. Are such arrangements practical, and for whom and when? You want to raise the subject of fiscal good sense through cost-effective programming and urge its persistence, when appropriate, in the future planning of your nonprofit collaborators.

You want to make certain that any dollar your foundation invests in a nonprofit organization enjoys maximum impact in changing the world.

CHAPTER 5

Between You and Your Board

Decisions, Recommendations and the Art of Communication

You have read the proposal, studied the budget, conducted the site visit. When an important item went missing—last year's financial statement, the IRS' certification of tax-exempt status, a plan for future funding—you contacted the proper person who then forwarded the final ingredients. When the applicant's assertions (on paper or in-person) struck you as cloudy, incomplete or incomprehensible, you requested clarification. In terms of evaluating the grant proposal, you are done.

Now is the moment that everybody has been waiting for. You must make a decision about funding, and then submit your recommendation to your board of directors so that they can take action. Or to state the situation in a slightly different way: You have entered yet another crucial and complicated area that will ultimately determine your effectiveness as a grantmaker.

Investing in the Common Good

As we have stressed throughout this book, the effective grantmaker must assume the role of ultimate middleman. You are the investment counselor, the deal maker, the person who fits all the pieces together and causes things to happen. It is important to take pleasure and pride in this role.

As a broker between nonprofit potential and critical funding resources, you will recognize how your grantmaking institution can serve as a catalyst to transform plans and visions into concrete achievements. You will introduce grantees to other grantees and during the years watch their relationship blossom into something none of you could have predicted from the start. With time, you will find yourself enjoying the justifiable satisfaction of participation with scores of projects.

In short, you will have learned how to assemble, manage and strengthen an array of grants that become, for all intents and purposes, a portfolio.

The Big Picture

Let us take a closer look at this concept of the grantmaker's "portfolio."

Enterprising and responsible funders do not judge their work on a grant-by-grant basis. Instead, they evaluate their entire roster of grants, embracing the long-term investor's view. Like the profit-making portfolio composed of assorted stocks and bonds ranging in various risk levels and potential payoffs, the grantmaker's portfolio strives for a balance and mix of investments for the common good. In sum, this carefully constructed portfolio also addresses your foundation's goals.

Many foundations, it should be noted, are not high risk takers. They tend toward the steady, dependable T-bill-variety of nonprofit investment that is often responsible for keeping essential services afloat. In recent years, however, more funders have recognized the need for seasoning their traditional support with more daring grants that offer the hope of some significant positive change for a community or a field. This tension between unglamorous necessities and alluring uncertainties is something that you must negotiate throughout your career.

Funders must also be aware of the external environment that shapes their grantmaking opportunities. Significant changes in your community (ranging from a natural disaster to a gradual, transformative shift in demography) may precipitate the need to temporarily "stretch" your guidelines. Occasionally, you will be approached by a visionary organization whose big plans and hefty budget represent an unanticipated chance to nudge the world into better shape with a decisive grant. Almost always, it will be up to you to identify these opportunities and counsel your board about their merits and liabilities in relation to your existing portfolio of grants.

Beyond preparing for the unexpected, the portfolio approach enables you to shift your grantmaking over time to achieve maximum progress in meeting long-range goals. If, for example, your board of directors has committed itself to improving the quality of youth programs for low-income families in your community, it may make sense to focus initially on grants to local youth centers. Later, with progress secured, you might consider broadening your portfolio by sponsoring a model center that embodies the best practices of the field or training for youth program directors. Still later, you may want to search out projects to influence national policy in the field or support research on why some youth development programs are more effective than others.

Balance, vision and varieties of opportunity and risk: these are the qualities that should characterize your grantmaking portfolio and help you nurture its development in collaboration with the members of your board.

Carrying Your Recommendations to the Board

All grantmaking institutions rely on the oversight of their boards. As the stewards of your foundation's vision and its endowment, your board members define and preserve the mission: they give final approval to all actions. In the end, they are accountable for the public disposition of the grants that you recommend to them in private.

Given this responsibility, you and the board must agree on the kinds of information they will receive about each proposal and the depth of analysis on each potential grant. Do not expect board demands to remain static. Over time, their appetite for detail may wax or wane; new members may inspire demands for additional information or dispense with traditional forms of analysis. Remain flexible. This ongoing negotiation is essential to your collaboration.

Generally, your written summaries should run one or two pages, three at most. Occasionally, board members will want to review entire proposals, although time considerations can temper such ambitions over time. Although there is no fast rule regarding the amount of detail your summaries should contain, you will want to strive for a common sense balance, neither overwhelming your board with paper nor starving them of essential and interesting content. Finally, the board must believe that it is receiving sufficient information from you to dispatch its duties and execute due diligence.

Beyond length, written recommendations also vary in intention, form and style. Some program officers outline the pros and cons of every grant, compelling the board to contrast potential benefits with prospective liabilities. Others have learned from experience that their board prefers a detailed oral defense of each recommendation, thereby instructing members in how projects adhere to the foundation's mission, goals and guidelines and how the approved grant will complement the existing portfolio.

Necessarily, the board meeting revisits essential questions about the priorities of your foundation or giving program, if only as the unstated basis for discussion. Once again, the grantmaker is thrown back on first principles: the clear and honest articulation of its mission. When a grantmaker lapses into vagueness regarding its funding goals, trouble is guaranteed.

To be fair, it is extremely difficult to move beyond the enticements of endless potential and decisively state what you stand for and stand against. Furthermore, foundation goals can, and should, change over time. Every few years, boards should return to their mission statements and review their priorities, exactly as they expect their grantees to do.

A final word about board approval. Getting 99 out of 100 recommendations approved by your board is not necessarily a good sign. It may mean that you have not offered them enough provocative proposals to test the limits of their vision. Your foundation may be mired in "safe" projects. Every now and then, you should gently prod the board into reconsidering its priorities in light of social, environmental, economic or political changes. Like you, the board should be scanning the nonprofit sector for new opportunities. In small foundations with a single professional staff person, it is especially important to play this demanding, but very constructive role. Friendly debate is a sign of health, a recognition that the conversation about funding aims, the root causes of social problems and the aspirations of philanthropy should never really come to an end.

Completing the Docket

Precisely what information should board members find in their grant summaries? Let us start with the basics.

Whether your board meets once, twice, four or even more times per year, they must quickly comprehend the basis of your recommendations. To this end, each grant recommendation summary should include the following:

1. A Brief Characterization of the Grant's Purpose

Explain the problem or issue addressed by the proposal and why it should interest your foundation. Summarize the operational strategy. Note any assumptions in the field of service or organizational milieu that will help the board grasp the proposal's more subtle implications. Explain exactly how your money will be spent, the geographic scope of the program and the timeline for beginning and ending.

2. A Cogent Sketch of the Sponsoring Organization

Describe the organization's background, outlining when and why it was founded. Explain its mission, its past achievements. Make the case for organizational credibility and capability. Tell who is running the organization as well as the specific project and how their skills align with the demands of the project. Include the names of key board members if they play an important role.

3. The Funding Context

Explain how this grant fits within your program guidelines. Strive to place your recommendations within the context of your foundation's grantmaking strategy. Defend your recommendation as an investment in the overall portfolio, a continuing acknowledgement of the pieces comprising the whole.

4. Financial Situation

Provide financial data to prove that the applicant organization is stable. Your board may request cash-flow statements, long-range funding plans or program-by-program financial statements. They may opt entirely for staff analysis, assuming due diligence on your part. In either case, the organization's financial health is the presumptive ante for board consideration unless you are funding new, grassroots or international organizations.

5. Your Personal Insights Regarding the Grant's Merits and Liabilities

Beyond summarizing material that appears in the proposal, you should also step back to offer your own personal take on each grant, adding the value of your burgeoning expertise, intuition and experience. Help the board members perceive how you have undertaken the review process; let them see the rightness of the recommendation through your eyes. You may also want to review any potential problems. Note the organizational weak links. Point out any potential public criticism that may result from the grant's approval.

These five items constitute the bare bones and sinews of your grant summaries. But there are other kinds of information that boards may reasonably wish to receive.

- With increasing frequency, boards want to be apprised of evaluation plans. How has this organization evaluated past efforts? Do their evaluations actually affect subsequent planning and program delivery? How will the group evaluate its proposed project? Does the evaluation component require supplemental funding?

- At times, an ambitious board with an appetite for analysis will even request a range of supporting materials, such as journal articles or newspaper accounts, to deepen their understanding of a particular field. If your board has recently committed to funding substance abuse programs, for example, its members may want to immerse themselves in the literature. Boards maintaining their traditional fields of interest might also depend on staff to provide them with materials that alert them to recent trends and developments.

- It will also be relevant and helpful to offer information on any prior relationship or previous grants made to the potential recipient of funds.

It Takes Time

How much time in advance of the meeting should board members receive their materials? Long enough to read everything and not so long that it will trickle out of memory. Ten days is about right. But again, you will need to negotiate the schedule with your board.

Keep in mind that staff needs sufficient time to conduct due diligence on each grant and then compose their recommendations. There is nothing pro-forma about this exercise. The quality of contact between board and staff—indeed, the ripeness of your recommendations and the eventual outcomes—may depend on the well-timed delivery of well-honed docket materials.

DOCKET TALK

So far we have been talking about the docket as though it were solely an accumulation of paper. In truth, the written materials merely constitute a departure point. During the board meeting, much will depend upon what you choose to say and how you say it. No matter how closely board members have studied the docket, their strongest impression—perhaps their ultimate decision about the disposition of a grant—may hinge upon your verbal rendition of its merits and liabilities.

Even if you reason like Euclid and construct prose that soars to Shakespearean heights, you will still need to cultivate strong presentation skills. That could mean mastering the latest computer-assisted audiovisual equipment, dispatching your life-long fear of public speaking or simply improving your verbal logic and expressive style so that you can relay a substantial amount of complex information with grace, inspiration and engaging good humor.

Bracing for Bad News

THE RISKINESS OF RECOMMENDATIONS

Eventually, it will happen. You will recommend a project, persuade your board to back you up and the project will fail. It will fail unequivocally and publicly. That does not necessarily mean you made a bad recommendation.

Failure occurs far more frequently than most people like to admit. Yet failure in any enterprise is often a necessary step in achieving eventual success. If it takes an organization three attempts to finally render an important service right, and you only fund attempt number two, it can still be argued that you have played an important developmental role. You may not share in the glory; but you can take legitimate pride in having provided essential backing during a critical period.

Then what is a bad recommendation? A bad recommendation is a poorly researched recommendation. A recommendation based on a cursory reading of a flawed proposal, a lackadaisical site visit, insufficient follow-up, attenuated vision. Bad recommendations are the product of presumption and neglected homework. Bad recommendations get made when you opt to follow other funders in their grantmaking practices, rather than determine if a proposal fits your foundation's mission and needs. The worst grants you make are not the absolute failures; you can learn from these. Rather, they are the programs that bumble along making little difference.

Bad recommendations may also be inevitable. You cannot always perform at the top of your game; you cannot see and know everything. You will make mistakes and so will your board.

Short of front-page scandals and grand jury investigations, it is not useful to perseverate on the occasional bad call. More important—we cannot say this too often—is the overall performance of your grantmaking portfolio.

Over months and years—in the aggregate—are you having the impact you desire? That is a much harder question to answer, requiring clear goals, careful investigation, mutually understood and agreed up expectations, analysis and honesty from all parties.

RISKY BUSINESS

More often than unequivocal failure, you will encounter the risky grant. The risks may reflect the potential for grand results, or they could be a lamentable but defining feature of the applicant organization. Whatever the case, you will at times face a sensitive decision. How should you inform your board of the risks?

If the board specifically asks for an appraisal of the downsides, then your decision is already made. You frankly outline the liabilities in their entirety.

Other cases prove murkier. What should you say to your board if you have vague, but nagging doubts about the capacity of the executive director who will oversee an otherwise fundable project? How should you explain your qualified support for a complicated project initiated by novices? What is the correct disclosure if you believe the applicant vastly misperceives its own potential, needs a better board to survive in the long run or any number of other bothersome and possibly tell-tale doubts?

More painfully, what do you do when you fall privy to a strict confidence, such as the fact that the very capable, experienced and esteemed executive director has decided to resign? What is your obligation to the person who gave you that piece of confidential information? To the applicant? To your own foundation and board?

There is no single right answer. Some boards frankly do not want to hear what may have been said to you in confidence. Instead, they will make their funding decisions based on visible externals: the organization's credibility, capability and your professional advice. They expect you to balance the pros and cons, bringing them recommendations where you believe that the potential benefits outweigh the risks.

Simply put, you and your board are stewards of the foundation's resources. Even though matters of confidentiality can present knotty dilemmas, and no true ethical dilemma is easy to resolve, you can make considerable progress by doing something rather daringly obvious. You can ask your board members what they want to know before it happens. Run through a range of hypotheticals—the doubtful budget, the departing executive—and learn from the board what it perceives to be your responsibility in terms of disclosure. You may still have close judgement calls to make now and then, but at least you will be working within a framework of reasonable, intelligible and explicit expectations.

Contact Paper

AWARD LETTERS AND REPORTS

Once your board has approved a grant, it is time to contact the applicant.

Your award letter does not simply serve as notification of the applicant's good fortune. It also formalizes your mutual agreement to collaborate on specific actions for a defined period. It is a restatement of commitments; a reminder of obligations and responsibilities; a contract. See Appendix to Chapter 5 for sample grant agreement letter.

The best award letters reiterate the objectives of the grant as you understand them and state whether the grant is restricted in some way. Make it clear that if you and the grantee differ in your interpretations, now is the time to speak. Discovering a difference in expectations early in the relationship can actually spark crucial discussion that will aid the project's eventual success. With the funds now approved, grantees may feel inclined to speak with greater frankness.

The nonprofit organization's authorizing agent—probably its executive director or board president—should be directed to sign and return a copy of the agreement. The explicit understanding: The check will quickly follow in the mail.

REPORTING BACK THE GOOD, THE BAD AND THE UNEXPECTED

Award letters should also stipulate your reporting requirements, outlining precisely what you want to know about the project's progress and when the information should be filed.

Be aware that reporting requirements constitute extra weight for most organizations—a burden that can handicap small organizations when it becomes too heavy. (Some of the weight can be mitigated by collaborating with other funders on the development and use of a common reporting form. Indeed, some models already exist. Your local regional association of grantmakers can point the way.) If for some defensible reason you require extensive evaluation procedures with loads of statistics and detailed analysis, make certain that you are also covering any extraordinary costs. To do otherwise undermines the organization's chances of success.

Nor should you exaggerate your own desire to study mounds of documents, graphs, tables and financial statements. Too copious reporting defeats its genuine purpose and it invites cynicism and exhaustion on both sides.

Then what is the report's true purpose? First, you and your board must learn how the money was spent. Quarterly or semiannual financial statements, along with a final financial report, should clearly provide this information.

Of equal importance, you will desire to know how the project fared: What was done? What problems were faced? What were the results? If the project is built around a set of specific objectives, then a brief narrative (three to five pages) should explain the progress in meeting them. Whatever your expectations, make the requirements clear to the grantee at the time the grant is made so that they can collect information throughout the project.

In the best of possible worlds, reporting will provide both the grantmaker and the grantee with a true portrait of activity: victories, potholes and everything else along the road. Reports should open channels of communication between grantee and grantmaker. Of course, this can only happen with established mutual trust. Too many reports qualify as works of historical fiction, composed to meet the presumed expectations of funders. It is up to you to define your grantees' reporting style, emphasizing your desire to read a few smartly written pages that will actually teach you something valuable about the nonprofit enterprise your foundation has already invested in.

Good reporting should inform your future grantmaking practices. Strive to persuade grantees that you would benefit from learning about unexpected outcomes or new knowledge gained. Indeed, you depend on reports from the field from your grantees; reiterations of the same old story will not help you grow in your role as grantmaker. Again, this can be a difficult case to make because many grantees believe that the unexpected disturbs grantmakers. But neat, simple stories are seldom found in the nonprofit sector. Open your ears to the subtle tales that truly reflect the reality of our efforts.

In short, let grantees know that you are always willing to entertain the same doubts, complexities and contradictions that they face daily—then move on together as partners to resolve them.

CHAPTER 6

Getting Better All the Time

Cultivating Professional Skills throughout Your Career

Good grantmaking takes time to master. Nobody expects you to step into your role with sterling skills and splendid insights. More reasonable expectations incline toward your long-term development—the cultivation of knowledge, poise, tenacity, discernment, vision and strategic dexterity. During months and years of conscious effort, taking pains to learn from both your successes and your failures, you will slowly grow to mastery.

How do you ensure your continuing development on the job? To begin, start with small, persistent efforts.

Take a Hard Look

In recent years, funders have correctly stressed the importance of engaging in program evaluation. Although nonprofits may sometimes feel burdened by these demands, their intent lies less in reassuring funders that grant money is being well-spent than in the crucial need for organizations to perceive the true measure of their effectiveness.

An equivalent demand for accountability should also be applied to grantmakers. After all, it is possible for a foundation to reap minimal results for years without undermining its stability or correcting its tactics. Foundations are endowed. They do not go out of business until the board decides it is time—a rare event. Grantmakers inhabit an unusually insular world that often proves too safe for their own good.

That means the responsibility for measuring your performance—both personal and institutional—rests squarely at your own feet.

One of the best ways to begin this process is to seize upon the habit of routine self-evaluation. In chapter 3, we discussed the value of debriefing after site visits. Such a practice not only provides guidance for new grantmakers; it also freshens the outlook of seasoned veterans. But site visits are not the only place to stage profitable reviews.

Another opportunity for surfacing thoughts and feelings about your own job performance resides at the conclusion of each quarterly board meeting. As board members digest your recommendations and then respond with their own questions, comments and objections, the work which you have previously conducted in the privacy of your office now becomes nakedly, vulnerably, perhaps even painfully public. This tender moment is the perfect time to ask yourself how you are doing on the job.

Of course, there is a natural temptation at this point to shy away from self-reflection. After all, board meetings can excavate long-buried conflict among the membership, with some of the pressure-packed debris landing directly on your toes. Yet it is precisely because board members must grapple with the essentials of mission and operations—What will we fund and why?—that you should afford yourself this opportunity for self-assessment.

Following the meeting, schedule 30 minutes for private contemplation. Return to your peaceful office. Pull out your pencil and notepad. Take a deep breath, exhale and then ask yourself the following:

- What did I add to our portfolio of grants during the past quarter?
- What went lacking?
- Did my docket summaries effectively convey the importance of each grant opportunity to the board?
- Did I provide the right information and documents?
- How might my presentation be more informative, interesting or helpful?
- Are there ways that I could have stimulated more constructive debate among board members?
- Am I presenting myself to the board effectively?
- Are my actions or intentions misperceived in any important way?
- Did I say anything that I wish I had not?
- What did I learn from the board meeting? How will it affect my future planning and actions?

Your self-evaluation will prove most advantageous if you do not rely entirely on your own feelings and intuition. Indeed, reflective moments are best leavened with hard data.

To this end, take some time to construct appropriate tables and graphs analyzing your recent grantmaking history. Try slicing the data in several different ways: by grant size, field of service, types of assistance, location, outcomes. Like the budget materials routinely submitted to you by grant applicants, this form of dispassionate analysis may end up stimulating your deeper, more subjective insights by highlighting the component parts of your grants portfolio and shaking out old complacent ways of thinking.

Other Tools for Other Times

Beyond reliance on your own insights, there are several established methods for reviewing grantmaking effectiveness that can ultimately improve your job performance and the overall performance of your foundation or corporate giving program.

To start, you might consider employing an outside evaluator. Because most grantmakers in single-staff offices enjoy scant opportunity to compare their procedures, decisions, goals and actions with those of their peers, it often falls upon an outsider to assume that rarest of philanthropic roles: the objective observer.

If you detect in yourself a reluctance to pursue this course, do not be surprised. Few people instinctively court criticism. (How many of us would ordinarily pay for an enumeration of our shortcomings?) Yet the fact that most of the individuals orbiting your foundation will duck any opportunity to submit an honest appraisal of your job performance is the very reason why you must solicit it.

Frankly, the risks involved are minimal. Nobody has to know that you are seeking professional help to ameliorate your shortcomings although everybody will notice the improvement. In fact, by asking for assistance, you are demonstrating your strength and flexibility, your seriousness and commitment. Regard the outside evaluator as a kind of personal trainer: an expert to coach you and your portfolio of grants into better shape.

Once you have hired your evaluator, be certain to allot sufficient time and access to render the effort practicable. Spend several hours together discussing your goals, strategies, actions. Provide an annotated list of grants. Hand over any analytical tools you have constructed.

In addition to inspecting the grant files, conducting interviews with you and your staff and closely observing the style and substance of your work, an outside evaluator can undertake a survey of grantees. On the most basic level, an evaluator can investigate consumer satisfaction: an anatomy of the ways in which grantseekers consider your philanthropic approach helpful or hindering. Keep in mind that the evaluator will be communicating with thoughtful people. You would not have invested in them if you did not approve of their work, their values or their capacity for critical thinking. Even rather mundane questions—"Were your phone calls returned in a timely fashion?"—may elicit useful feedback that cuts to the core of your grantmaking style.

Beyond the process evaluation, ask your consultant to pursue a more philosophical inquiry. Ask grantees to talk about what you still need to learn about their organization, their field, philanthropy in general. Ask what your foundation should consider doing that it has not yet attempted. What are the big issues, obstacles and opportunities that grantees foresee in your community and our society at-large? Most important in working with an outside evaluator, push for unambiguous insights. Let the evaluator know that at the end of this process, you want to be provided with at least three suggestions for improving your grantmaking. Then act on whatever advice you deem feasible and wise.

A variation on this theme of outsider estimation is the panel of advisors. A probing visit by experts can provoke lively dialogue and will almost certainly surface new ideas which may lead you to a fresh approach.

Evaluation of a Grantmaker (excerpt)

While many people in the philanthropic community are talking about "evaluation" these days, the term is usually used to ask: What can we do to measure the effectiveness of the organizations and programs to which we give money? As grantmakers, we should also ask: How can we examine the effectiveness of our own grantmaking programs?

Burnett, Mara E. and Ford, David S. "Evaluation of a Grantmaker." *Foundation News & Commentary*, January/February 1996, p. 46.

Mara E. Burnett is a consultant for nonprofits and grantmakers. David S. Ford is director of Philanthropy for Chase Manhattan Bank, New York City.

Benchmarking

Another means of charting your own job performance is to compare your achievements with the accomplishments of other grantmaking institutions. Start off this exercise by identifying a half-dozen foundations of a size and scale similar to your own. Search for a good fit between your organizations' programs and goals, a congruence of fundamental aspirations. Then schedule a visit. Learn everything you can about your peer's daily operations, strategies and methods for formulating long-range goals and measuring progress in meeting them. Find out how your peers gauge improvements in their relationships with grantees and advance their own professional development. In other words, use the same skills of investigation and observation—hard questioning and dogged listening—that you have practiced innumerable times in the past during site visits with prospective grantees.

As you come to understand more about how other foundations make their decisions to award or deny grants, you will doubtlessly find practices to admire and emulate and others to avoid. Gradually, you will recognize where you stand in relation to the rest of the philanthropic community. Both positive and negative examples will help you to measure your own performance.

THE POWER OF PROFESSIONAL DEVELOPMENT

All of these methods for self-evaluation in pursuit of self-improvement hinge upon a common factor: your willingness to break with the office routine, step out from behind your desk and learn to see yourself as others see you. But the task does not end there. Now it is time to construct a strategy for self-improvement.

In most cases, it will be up to you to allocate funds for professional development in your annual operating budget. Beyond the costs of hiring outside evaluators, you may want to set aside some funds each year to purchase books and publications, enroll in workshops and classes and hire consultants to sharpen your skills in the areas that you now know need improvement.

For some grantmakers, it may prove easier to loosen purse strings and work hours if professional development is framed by the formality of written annual goals. Once you have identified your weaker skills, you can outline the necessary steps to strengthening them. Whenever possible, tie your actions to realistic calendar dates.

If, for example, you know on the first day of January that you want to improve your presentation skills in the coming year, resolve to read an excellent book on the subject by the first day of February. If you are still not satisfied with your knowledge, schedule two days of consultation with a local expert during the middle of the month. By the time you conduct your first-quarter self-review, you should be able to tell if you are making progress toward your goal.

As a grantmaker, you can improve as much or as little as you desire; that is one of the great benefits of the job and one of its unremitting responsibilities. Professional growth depends largely on your own initiative. Consider the athlete in perpetual training, the accomplished musician who never ceases study with a master teacher. That is the ethic you should strive for: dynamic, patient, purposeful effort dedicated over the long-run to achieving professional excellence.

Your Ultimate Balancing Act

You toss one ball up in the air, catch another as it is falling. All the while, you are brightly whistling something witty and complex from Brahms or Bach and traveling the winding route to your next appointment. Somehow the balls do not drop to the ground and scatter at your feet.

Some days that is exactly what it feels like to be a grantmaker. Most of the time, you handle it all with a smile on your face, hoping to please the audience while deftly doing some good in the world that might not always get noticed.

The grantmaker as juggler: a challenging, exhilarating job that is frequently an adventure. Most of the time it is lots of fun. That is something we should not forget. Despite all the sweat and struggle involved in becoming an effective grantmaker, the results justify the effort.

Throughout the course of this book, we have outlined the skills and information you will need to get started on the job. But in the end, there is no one right way to become an effective professional. Over time, you will develop your own style. You will discover your own means of helping good things to grow. You may even learn how to collaborate with other productive people in the nonprofit world in ways that nobody else has yet attempted. Inevitably, you will build strengths and skills that complement your own personality, interests and inclinations. You will cull insights from your efforts and you will gain perspective from your experience. Then you will take what you have learned and pass it along to the next person you meet who is bravely and expectantly stepping into the exciting world of grantmaking that you have now come to regard as home.

Consulting with Peers

Consultation with your peers is a good means of exploring the complicated contextual issues that lie beneath the surface of much grantmaking today. Unless you only fund projects in an unusually homogeneous community—a place characterized by uniformity of race, class, culture, national origin and language—then you will need to become conversant with a variety of institutions, attitudes, cultural traditions and histories that may elude your present understanding. This is not an argument for political correctness or a knee-jerk deference to the unfamiliar. Rather, it is a common sense recommendation that you acquaint yourself with the communities you serve—a tall order as we begin the 21st century. That is why your more experienced peers—the people in other foundations who have been doing what you do longer—should be consulted when you encounter a new funding opportunity that appears both promising and perplexing.

Ask: Who should I talk with to learn more about the emerging sources of power in our community? What books should I read about other cultures? What events should I attend, what periodicals should I scroll through weekly?

Appendix to Chapter 1

For 50 years, the Council on Foundations has helped foundation staff, trustees and board members in their day-to-day grantmaking activities. Through one-to-one technical assistance, research, publications, conferences and workshops, legal services, and a wide array of other services, the Council addresses the important issues and challenges that face foundations and corporate funders.

Council members include more than 1,800 grantmaking organizations, such as

- Community Foundations
- Corporate Foundations/Giving Programs
- Family Foundations
- Private Operating Foundations
- Private Independent Foundations
- Public Foundations
- International Programs

Other programs and services include

- Research
- Promoting Inclusive Practices

Council on Foundations
1828 L Street, NW
Washington, DC 20036
202/466-6512

For more information, contact **www.cof.org**.
(material taken from Council on Foundations Web site)

Council on Foundations Affinity Groups

Affinity groups and grantmaker associations represent a variety of different issues and population groups. They are a source for up-to-date grantmaking information in their areas of interest. Some groups emphasize networking and information exchange among members, while others advocate for an issue or cause within philanthropy and beyond. Generally, these groups serve the grantmaking community, although some include grantee organizations as members. The typical group is a network managed by volunteers, although a growing number are becoming nonprofit organizations in their own right.

The variety of these organizations provides rich resources for Council members and others. Many foundations that are Council members are also members of one or more affinity groups. This list is intended for grantmakers and trustees seeking a greater understanding of a particular area of philanthropy.

Affinity Group on Japanese Philanthropy

Asian Americans/Pacific Islanders in Philanthropy

Association of Black Foundation Executives

Association of Small Foundations

The Communications Network

Disability Funders Network

Environmental Grantmakers Association

Forum on Religion, Philanthropy and Public Life

Funders' Committee for Citizen Participation

Funders Concerned about AIDS

Grantmaker Forum on Community and National Service

Grantmakers Concerned with Care at the End of Life

Grantmakers Concerned with Immigrants and Refugees

Grantmakers Evaluation Network

Grantmakers for Children, Youth and Families

Grantmakers for Education

Grantmakers for Effective Organizations

Grantmakers for Public Safety

Grantmakers in Aging

Grantmakers in Film and Electronic Media

Grantmakers in Health

Grantmakers in the Arts

Grantmakers Income Security Task Force

Grants Managers Network

Harm Reduction Funders' Network

Hispanics in Philanthropy

Jewish Funders Network

National Network of Grantmakers

National Office on Philanthropy and the Black Church

Native Americans in Philanthropy

Neighborhood Funders Group

Southern Africa Grantmakers

Technology Affinity Group

Women & Philanthropy

Women's Funding Network

Working Group on Funding Lesbian and Gay Issues

For more information, check out **www.cof.org/links/affinityindex.htm**.
(material taken from Council on Foundations Web site)

Regional Associations of Grantmakers (RAGs)

As grantmakers look to maximize their impact in today's challenging and exciting nonprofit environment, they have joined forces in growing numbers to form RAGs for the purpose of promoting effective philanthropy in their areas. RAGs began forming as early as the late 1940s. Today, more than 3,200 grantmakers of all types belong to one or more of the approximately 50 RAGs across the United States. The 29 largest of these RAGs belong to the national Forum of Regional Associations of Grantmakers.

Regional associations of grantmakers—RAGs—are nonprofit membership associations of grantmakers and related organizations that share a common goal: to strengthen philanthropy in a distinct geographic region—be it a city, state or multistate area.

RAG members include private or independent foundations, community foundations and corporate foundations and giving programs. In addition, some RAGs include in their membership other related organizations, such as financial advisor firms or nonprofit grantseeking groups. The number of members and even types of eligible members vary.

RAGs have been set up by their members to provide a variety of services to grantmakers and the public alike. No single description fits all—or even most—RAGs. How a RAG develops depends on its leadership, the public context in which it operates, its audiences, the philanthropy in its area of service, and most of all its member grantmakers.

Individual RAGs accomplish their goals through varied efforts that include

- facilitating and increasing communication and information-sharing among members.
- alerting members to community needs and emerging issues in philanthropy.
- enhancing the effectiveness of members' decisionmaking, and their use of philanthropic resources.
- encouraging the development of new philanthropy.
- promoting sound public policy on issues affecting philanthropy and the nonprofit sector.
- improving grantmaker-grantseeker cooperation and communication.
- initiating, leading and facilitating collaborations and new approaches to solving community problems.

For more information, contact **www.rag.org**.
(material taken from Forum of Regional Associations of Grantmakers Web site)

Appendix to Chapter 2

Proposal Review Worksheet | Notes

1. **What** is the applicant organization proposing to do?

    a. What are its goals?

    b. Are its proposed activities likely to achieve these goals?

    c. Beyond the stated goals, what other changes are likely to occur by the project's end?

    d. Does the proposal clearly describe and justify the project's ongoing activities?

    e. Does it offer insights into how the project will be structured, staffed and managed?

2. **Why** is this project being proposed?

    a. What needs does it address?

    b. What evidence establishes the existence of these needs?

    c. Are these needs important?

    d. What kinds of benefits will be derived from the project's implementation?

    e. Are any unintended positive (or negative) effects likely?

3. **Where** will the project take place?

    a. Why was this area selected?

    b. Will the project have influence or repercussions elsewhere?

4. **When** will the project take place?

   a. What is the timeline for accomplishing the work?

   b. Is the timeline realistic?

   c. Are there any crucial deadlines that must be met?

   d. Is the organization capable of keeping to the timeline and meeting its deadlines?

5. **Who** will participate in the project?

   a. Who will the program serve?

   b. Are they the right target group given the project's goals?

   c. Who will provide the services?

   d. What are their capabilities?

   e. Who will oversee the project?

   f. What are their qualifications?

   g. Is anybody else attempting similar projects?

   h. Is a consultation, collaboration or alliance with other organizations being considered? If not, why?

6. **How** are the chances of success being maximized?

   a. Is the project's approach practical?

   b. Does it demonstrate an understanding of best practices in the field?

   c. Have other organizations gotten results by using equivalent means?

   d. Are you aware of similar programs that have run into serious problems in the past?

   e. Are there any crucial difficulties the proposal has not anticipated?

   f. How will success be measured?

7. **How much** will the project cost?

   a. Is the budget adequate to carry out the program?

   b. Has the budget been padded to absorb unrelated expenses?

   c. Is the organization using any of its unrestricted resources to support the project?

   d. Have other funders committed their support?

   e. How will the project continue after your funding is over?

Notes

Appendix to Chapter 3

Grantmaker Jeopardy
A Quick Reference Guide to Successful Interviews

PLANNING

YOU WANT TO KNOW...	*DO NOT* ASK...	*DO* ASK...
...if the organization is flexible and able to cope with rapid change.	Are you capable of planning for unforeseen contingencies?	We are all working in a rapidly changing environment where many things that affect us are outside of our control. What are the challenges you see ahead for your organization? How are you planning to prepare for or address these challenges?
...if the organization's leaders are aware of the larger context of their work.	Do you know what is going on in your field?	What are some of the external resources/tools that you rely on in your work? How are you linking with colleagues in the field?
...if the organization's statement of purpose reflects what it actually does.	Does your organization's purpose statement describe what you actually do?	From your perspective, what does your organization's overall statement of purpose mean for you, your work and the work of the organization? What is its relevance to the day-to-day work?
...if, in general, the organization achieves what it sets out to do.	Do you actually achieve what you set out to do?	What were some of the key goals set for your program during the past year? What recent accomplishments are you most proud of? Why?
...if the organization pays adequate attention to overall planning.	Do you plan?	How do you, your board and your colleagues make decisions about the overall direction of your organization?

Grantmaker Jeopardy
A Quick Reference Guide to Successful Interviews

GOVERNANCE

YOU WANT TO KNOW...	DO NOT ASK...	DO ASK...
...if board/staff relations are good. AND ...if the respective roles of board and staff are defined and honored.	Do staff and board work well together? OR Does your board know its place?	The roles of the board and board/staff relationships are among the most challenging aspects of organizational life. What are the issues your board is dealing with right now? How are board and staff working together, and separately, to address these issues?
...if the committee structure is aligned with the core functions and challenges facing the organization.	Does your committee structure make sense?	How is the board organized to do its work? If there are committees, what are the core responsibilities of each? What are some of the ways that each board committee has been most helpful? Least helpful?
...if the board assesses its own performance periodically.	Does the board think about what it is doing?	What are the board's goals for its own performance? How are these goals developed and reviewed?
...if there is adequate attention to board development/training.	Does the board know what it is doing?	How are new board members oriented to the organization and to their role on the board? What else is done to keep the board refreshed, committed and capable over time?
...if the relationship between the executive director and the chair of the board is strong.	Do you get along with...?	How would you describe your relationship with...? In what ways could the relationship be improved?

Grantmaker Jeopardy
A Quick Reference Guide to Successful Interviews

STAFF CAPABILITIES AND MORALE

YOU WANT TO KNOW...	*DO NOT* ASK...	DO ASK...
...if the staff leadership of the proposed program/project are qualified and capable.	Are your staff qualified to direct and implement this program?	A capable staff is essential to a successful program but it can be very hard to find and train the right people. Tell me about the background of key staff? What do you see as their greatest strengths?
...if staff morale is good.	How is staff morale?	Stress seems to be everywhere these days and you are running a challenging and ambitious program. What are the most stressful aspects of your work right now? How are you and your staff coping with these stresses?
...if staff turnover is high.	Have you experienced high turnover on the staff recently?	How long has each of your team members been with the program?
...how the staff view the board.	Do you think the board knows what it is doing?	What are some of the ways in which the board supports staff and vice versa?
...if there is adequate attention to staff training and development.	Is the staff trained to do their work?	Are you able to offer professional development opportunities for staff? What additional staff development would you offer if resources were not an issue?
...if the executive director is respected by her or his subordinates.	Do you respect your boss?	What are some of the key strengths of the executive director? What are some of the areas where she or he could use some extra help, support or training?

Appendix to Chapter 3

Grantmaker Jeopardy
A Quick Reference Guide to Successful Interviews

PROGRAM STRENGTH/POTENTIAL IMPACT

YOU WANT TO KNOW...	*DO NOT* ASK...	DO ASK...
...why the applicant has chosen a particular approach to an issue and whether the program leaders are aware of best practices in the field.	Are you aware of best practices in the field?	What was your process for researching and designing your particular approach to this program? What were some of the reasons for selecting this approach?
...if the applicant organization is in touch with and responsive to its community and constituents.	Is your organization responsive to its constituents?	What are some of your strategies for getting input from your clients/constituents? What do your clients/constituents think are the most important needs/issues?
...if the organization considers input from constituencies in planning and decisionmaking.	Do you pay attention to your clients' point of view?	How do you use input from your clients/constituents in making decisions about your programs/operations?
...if the agency's programs actually produce an acceptable level of quality services. AND ...if there is appropriate attention to evaluation overall.	Is your program of the highest quality? OR Do you evaluate your programs?	With all the pressures to deliver services, it is often very hard to find the time and resources to reflect on what has happened in the past. Are you able to invest any time/resources in evaluation right now? If yes, what kinds of information do you find meaningful in reflecting on the impact of your work? How do you get this information? How is it useful to you? If no, what are some of the barriers you face regarding evaluation?

Site Visit Worksheet

Purpose of/Rationale for Site Visit: _____

_____

I. Preparing for the Visit

Organization: _____ _____ Time and Date of Visit: _____

Address: _____

_____

Phone: _____

Directions: _____

_____

Summary of the request _____

_____

Preliminary analysis of proposal:

Strengths +	Weaknesses −

Appendix to Chapter 3

Questions raised:

_____

_____

_____

Other information or assumptions about organization:

_____

_____

_____

_____

II. Field Notes

Persons interviewed (name/title): _____

Impressions or Observations of:

- Physical plant (Prompts: Do they appear to have the infrastructure necessary to accomplish what they propose in their request?): _____
_____
_____

- Staff (Prompts: Do they appear to be adequately staffed? Does the staff appear to be motivated and engaged in their work?): _____
_____
_____

- Other: _____
_____
_____

General questions/prompts:

- What are the trends you see coming?
- What special challenges are ahead for you/your organization?
- Within your organization?
- Financially?
- Concerning your clients/constituents?
- Who else is doing good work in your field?
- What else would you like me to know?
- Do you have any questions for me? _____
_____
_____

Reminder: Be sure to . . .

- Explain the review and approval process.
- Confirm next steps. (What will they do? What will you do?)
- Establish a timeline for review and decision. _____
_____
_____

III. Debrief

What are my overall impressions of this organization?

What was learned during the site visit?

What questions remain?

What new issues emerged?

What else do I need to know to make a decision on the request?

What are my next steps?

How can I improve my next site visit?

Appendix to Chapter 5

Grant Recommendations Summary Template

Grantee Name: _____

Amount of Recommendation: _____

I. Request:

A brief statement of how the funds would be used.

II. Prior Grants:

A summary of your history with this grantseeker.

III. Background:

A brief paragraph or two that establishes the credibility of the grantseeker and the importance of the need to be addressed through the grant.

IV. Specific Objectives:

A summary of the key tasks and hoped-for outcomes of the project or program to be supported.

V. Evaluation:

Highlights of the grantseeker's plans to document the process and demonstrate the impact of the proposed project or program.

VI. Finance:

A brief statement concerning the grantseeker's financial stability and/or discussion of the projected expenses and revenues for the program.

VII. Personnel (Board and Staff):

Background on the relevant experience and expertise of key staff and volunteers.

VIII. Staff Analysis:

Arguably the most important part of the summary recommendation is the staff's analysis of the potential benefits and risks of making the grant. This miniessay should also clearly establish how the grant fits with your foundation or corporate giving program's goals and funding priorities.

Sample Grant Agreement for Grants to Public Charities

[DATE]

Dear [CONTACT NAME]:

Enclosed is the [NAME] Foundation's ("Foundation") check for $[AMOUNT] to [GRANTEE'S FULL NAME] ("Grantee"). This constitutes a grant to support Grantee's [DESCRIBE ACTIVITY OR INSERT NAME OF PROJECT].

This grant is made by Foundation subject to the following terms and conditions:

(a) Grantee is an organization that is both exempt from tax under section 501(c)(3) of the Internal Revenue Code (IRC) and an organization described in IRC §509(a)(1), (2), or (3), which statuses have been duly confirmed by one or more operative IRS rulings or determination letters, copies of which Grantee has filed with Foundation.

(b) Grantee will utilize the grant's proceeds only for charitable and educational activities consistent with its tax-exempt status described above. Without limiting the generality of the preceding sentence, Grantee will not intervene in any election or support or oppose any political party or candidate for public office, or engage in any lobbying not permitted by IRC §501(c)(3) or, if applicable, IRC §501(h) and 4911.

(c) Grantee will inform Foundation immediately of any change in or IRS proposed or actual revocation (whether or not appealed) of its tax status described above.

(d) Grantee will report in writing to Foundation by [date and year] (and each subsequent [date and year], when pertinent) as to the uses it has put Foundation's grant and will provide promptly such additional information, reports and documents as Foundation may request.

Foundation, select either Option 1 or Option 2

Option 1 (for general support grants):

(e) This is a general support grant. It is not earmarked for any project or for transmittal to any other entity or person, even if Grantee's proposal or other correspondence expresses expenditure intentions. Rather, Grantee accepts and will discharge full control of the grant and its disposition and responsibility for complying with this agreement's terms and conditions.

Option 2 (for project grants):

(e) This grant is earmarked for the project identified above, as described in Grantee's funding proposal and related correspondence. It is not earmarked for transmittal to any other entity or person, even if Grantee's proposal or other correspondence expresses expenditure intentions. Rather, Grantee accepts and will discharge full control of the grant and its disposition and responsibility for complying with this agreement's terms and conditions.

(f) This grant is not in any way earmarked to support or carry on any lobbying or voter-registration drive. If this grant is restricted to a specific project, Grantee hereby reaffirms that the project's current budget, as previously submitted or explained to Foundation, accurately reflects Grantee's present intentions to expend at least the amount of this grant (plus any other grant from the Foundation this year for the same project) on project non-lobbying and non-voter-registration activities in Grantee's current fiscal year.

Grantee's deposit, negotiation or endorsement of the enclosed check will constitute its agreement to the terms and conditions set forth above. However, for Foundation's files, please have the enclosed copy of this letter reviewed and signed where indicated by an authorized officer of Grantee and then returned to us at your earliest convenience.

Sincerely,

Executive Director

On behalf of grantee, I understand and agree to the foregoing terms and conditions of Foundation's grant, and hereby certify my authority to executive this agreement on Grantee's behalf.

Signature: _____

Name: _____
      (TYPE OR PRINT)

Title: _____

Date: _____

Asher, Thomas R. *Myth v. Fact: Foundation Support of Advocacy.* A Publication of the Alliance for Justice; 1995. *Reprinted with permission.*

Sample of Reporting Letter

[DATE]

Dear [CONTACT NAME]:

Congratulations on your recent grant from [grantmaking organization]. This grant, in the amount of $[amount], is made through the [program area, if applicable] and is meant for support for [project title]. You should have *received (or Shortly, you will receive)* formal notice of this award from the Foundation. This letter outlines the reporting requirements of this grant.

Your grant has a final (*interim, if applicable*) report due on [DATE REPORT DUE]. We understand from your proposal that this project has the following objectives: [LIST OBJECTIVES]. We would like you to address these objectives specifically in your report. If your understanding of the project objectives is not the same as ours, please contact me so that we may clarify them. Please keep us informed of any significant modifications to these objectives during the project period.

Every grant is a learning opportunity, both for the grantee and for the Foundation. Your final report is an opportunity to reflect upon the project's challenges and successes. Our greatest interest is in learning about the insight you have gained from undertaking your project. Few projects go exactly as planned, but any project can strengthen an organization if learning occurs. Your candor will help us to increase our understanding of the current and evolving challenges facing our grantees and the strategies they are using to overcome them.

We are pleased that [GRANTEE NAME] has chosen to undertake this project and look forward to learning from your progress and successes. Feel free to call if you have questions or require further clarification of our reporting procedures. We also welcome your feedback; if you have suggestions about ways in which the Foundation might improve its [PROGRAM AREA, IF APPLICABLE], we invite you to share those observations with us at any time.

Sincerely,

[FOUNDATION CONTACT NAME]

Note: If you wish any specific reporting requirements to be binding on the grantee, it is advisable to incorporate your requirements into the grant agreement letter.

FOUNDATION NAME
REPORTING GUIDELINES

Grantee Name: [GRANTEE NAME]   **Grant Number:** [GRANT NUMBER]

Report Due: Final Report—[DATE REPORT DUE]   **Award Date:** [AWARD DATE]

Please Note:

- Include with your report a detailed financial accounting of all grant funds.
- Kindly refer to your grant number in all correspondence with the Foundation.
- Your report should address each of the items below. Answers need not be lengthy; three to five pages for the report is often adequate.

Project Objectives:
[LIST OBJECTIVES]

General Questions:
Interim Report: *(if applicable)*

1. What challenges are you facing as you move forward with this project? How are you approaching these challenges?
2. Have you revised your original objectives since the project began? If so, why? What are your new objectives?
3. What progress have you made toward achieving your objectives? Please address each stated objective.
4. Do you anticipate any difficulties in completing your project in the timeframe outlined in your proposal?

Final Report:

1. What was accomplished in connection with this project? Please address each stated objective. If any project objectives were changed, please also explain the circumstances leading to the modification of the objective(s).
2. What challenges did you face in connection with this project? How did you address these challenges?
3. What were the most important lessons learned?
4. What has changed within your organization as a result of this project?
5. What advice would you offer to help another organization that is thinking about undertaking a similar project?

Appendix to Chapter 6

Board Meeting Self-Evaluation

Following the Board meeting, schedule 30 minutes for private contemplation.

What did I add to our portfolio of grants over the past quarter? _____

_____

What went lacking? _____

Did my docket summaries effectively convey the importance of each grant opportunity to the board? _____

_____

Did I provide the right information and documents? _____

_____

How might my presentation be more informative; interesting; helpful? _____

_____

Are there ways that I could have stimulated more constructive debate among board members? _____

_____

Am I presenting myself to the board effectively? _____

_____

Are my actions or intentions misperceived in any important way? _____

_____

Did I say anything that I wish I had not? _____

_____

What did I learn from the board meeting? How will it affect my future planning and actions? _____

_____

Glossary

501(c)(3):

Section of the Internal Revenue Code that designates an organization as charitable and tax-exempt. Organizations qualifying under this section include religious, educational, charitable, amateur athletic, scientific or literary groups, organizations testing for public safety or organizations involved in prevention of cruelty to children or animals. Most organizations seeking foundation or corporate contributions secure a Section 501(c)(3) classification from the Internal Revenue Service (IRS).

Note: The tax code sets forth a list of sections—501(c)(4-26)—to identify other nonprofit organizations whose function is not solely charitable (e.g., professional or veterans organizations, chambers of commerce, fraternal societies, etc.).

509(a):

Section of the tax code that defines public charities (as opposed to private foundations). A 501(c)(3) organization also must have a 509(a) designation to further define the agency as a public charity. (See **Public Support Test**.)

Affinity Group:

A separate and independent coalition of grantmaking institutions or individuals associated with such institutions that shares information or provides professional development and networking opportunities to individual grantmakers with a shared interest in a particular subject or funding area.

Annual Report:

A voluntary report published by a foundation or corporation describing its grant activities. It may be a simple, typed document listing the year's grants or an elaborately detailed publication. A growing number of foundations and corporations use an annual report as an effective means of informing the community about their contributions activities, policies and guidelines. (The annual contributions report is not to be confused with a corporation's annual report to the stockholders.)

Articles of Incorporation:

A document filed with the secretary of state or other appropriate state office by persons establishing a corporation. This is the first legal step in forming a nonprofit corporation.

Assets:

Cash, stocks, bonds, real estate or other holdings of a foundation. Generally, assets are invested and the income is used to make grants. (See **Payout Requirement**.)

Bequest:

A sum of money made available upon the donor's death.

"Bricks and Mortar":

An informal term indicating grants for buildings or construction projects.

Building Campaign:

A drive to raise funds for construction or renovation of buildings.

Bylaws:

Rules governing the operation of a nonprofit corporation. Bylaws often provide the methods for the selection of directors, the creation of committees and the conduct of meetings.

Capital Campaign:

Also referred to as a Capital Development Campaign, a capital campaign is an organized drive to collect and accumulate substantial funds to finance major needs of an organization such as a building or major repair project.

Challenge Grant:

A grant that is made on the condition that other monies must be secured, either on a matching basis or via some other formula, usually within a specified period of time, with the objective of stimulating giving from additional sources.

Charity:

In its traditional legal meaning, the word "charity" encompasses religion, education, assistance to the government, promotion of health, relief of poverty or distress and other purposes that benefit the community. Nonprofit organizations that are organized and operated to further one of these purposes generally will be recognized as exempt from federal income tax under Section 501(c)(3) of the Internal Revenue Code (see **501(c)(3)**) and will be eligible to receive tax-deductible charitable gifts.

Community Foundation:

A community foundation is a tax-exempt, nonprofit, autonomous, publicly supported, philanthropic institution composed primarily of permanent funds established by many separate donors of the long-term diverse, charitable benefit of the residents of a defined geographic area. Typically, a community foundation serves an area no larger than a state.

Community foundations provide an array of services to donors who wish to establish endowed funds without incurring the administrative and legal costs of starting independent foundations. There are more than 500 community foundations across the United States today. The Cleveland Foundation is the oldest; the New York Community Trust is the largest. Examples of recently started, thriving community foundations include the Community Foundation for the Fox Valley Region, Wisconsin, and the Delaware Community Foundation.

Corporate Foundation:

A corporate (company-sponsored) foundation is a private foundation that derives its grantmaking funds primarily from the contributions of a profit-making business. The company-sponsored foundation often maintains close ties with the donor company, but it is a separate, legal organization, sometimes with its own endowment, and is subject to the same rules and regulations as other private foundations. There are more than 2,000 corporate foundations in the United States holding some $11 billion in assets. (See **Corporate Giving Program**.)

Corporate Giving Program:

A corporate giving (direct giving) program is a grantmaking program established and administered within a profit-making company. Gifts or grants go directly to charitable organizations from the corporation. Corporate foundations/giving programs do not have a separate endowment; their expense is planned as part of the company's annual budgeting process and usually is funded with pre-tax income. The Foundation Center has identified more than 700 corporate foundations/giving programs in the United States; however, it is believed that several thousand are in operation.

Decline:

Also referred to as Denial, a decline is the refusal or rejection of a grant request. Some declination letters explain why the grant was not made, but many do not.

Demonstration Grant:

A grant made to establish an innovative project or program that will serve as a model, if successful, and may be replicated by others.

Designated Funds:

A type of restricted fund in which the fund beneficiaries are specified by the grantors.

Discretionary Funds:

Grant funds distributed at the discretion of one or more trustees, which usually do not require prior approval by the full board of directors. The governing board can delegate discretionary authority to staff.

Disqualified Person: (Private Foundation)

Substantial contributors to a private foundation, foundation managers, certain public officials, family members of disqualified persons and corporations and partnerships in which disqualified persons hold significant interests. The law bars most financial transactions between disqualified persons and foundations. (See **Self-Dealing**.)

Disqualified Person: (Public Charity)

As applied to public charities, the term disqualified person includes (1) organization managers, (2) and any other person who, within the past five years, was in a position to exercise substantial influence over the affairs of the organization, (3) family members of the above, and (4) businesses they control. Paying excessive benefits to a disqualified person will result in the imposition of penalty excise taxes on that person, and, under some circumstances, on the charity's board of directors (See **Intermediate Sanctions**.)

Donee:

See **Grantee**.

Donor:

See **Grantor**.

Donor Advised Fund:

A fund held by a community foundation where the donor, or a committee appointed by the donor, may recommend eligible charitable recipients for grants from the fund. The community foundation's governing body must be free to accept or reject the recommendations.

Donor Designated Fund:

A fund held by a community foundation where the donor has specified that the fund's income or assets be used for the benefit of one or more specific public charities. These funds are sometimes established by a transfer of assets by a public charity to a fund designated for its own benefit, in which case they may be known as grantee endowments. The community foundation's governing body must have the power to redirect resources in the fund if it determines that the donor's restriction is unnecessary, incapable of fulfillment or inconsistent with the charitable needs of the community or area served.

Endowment:

The principal amount of gifts and bequests that are accepted subject to a requirement that the principal be maintained intact and invested to create a source of income for a foundation. Donors may require that the principal remain intact in perpetuity, or for a defined period of time or until sufficient assets have been accumulated to achieve a designated purpose.

Excise Tax:

The annual tax of 1 or 2 percent of net investment income that must be paid to the IRS by private foundations.

Expenditure Responsibility:

When a private foundation makes a grant to an organization that is not classified by the IRS as tax-exempt under Section 501(c)(3) and as a public charity according to Section 509(a), it is required by law to ensure that the funds are spent for charitable purposes and not for private gain or political activities. Such grants require a pre-grant inquiry and a detailed, written agreement. Special reports on the status of the grant must be filed with the IRS, and the grantees must be listed on the foundation's IRS Form 990-PF.

Family Foundation:

"Family foundation" is not a legal term, and therefore, it has no precise definition.
Yet, approximately two-thirds of the estimated 44,000 private foundations in this country are believed to be family managed. The Council on Foundations defines a family foundation as a foundation whose funds are derived from members of a single family. At least one family member must continue to serve as an officer or board member of the foundation, and as the donor, they or their relatives play a significant role in governing and/or managing the foundation throughout its life. Most family foundations are run by family members who serve as trustees or directors on a voluntary basis—receiving no compensation; in many cases, second- and third-generation descendants of the original donors manage the foundation. Most family foundations concentrate their giving locally, in their communities.

Field of Interest Fund:

A fund held by a community foundation that is used for a specific charitable purpose such as education or health research.

Financial Report:

An accounting statement detailing financial data, including income from all sources, expenses, assets and liabilities. A financial report may also be an itemized accounting that shows how grant funds were used by a donee organization. Most foundations require a financial report from grantees.

Form 990/Form 990-PF:

The IRS forms filed annually by public charities and private foundations respectively. The letters PF stand for private foundation. The IRS uses this form to assess compliance with the Internal Revenue Code. Both forms list organization assets, receipts, expenditures and compensation of officers. Form 990-PF includes a list of grants made during the year by private foundations.

Funding Cycle:

A chronological pattern of proposal review, decisionmaking and applicant notification. Some donor organizations make grants at set intervals (quarterly, semi-annually, etc.), while others operate under an annual cycle.

Giving Pattern:

The overall picture of the types of projects and programs that a donor has supported historically. The past record may include areas of interest, geographic locations, dollar amount of funding or kinds of organizations supported.

Grant:

An award of funds to an organization or individual to undertake charitable activities.

Grant Monitoring:

The ongoing assessment of the progress of the activities funded by a donor, with the objective of determining if the terms and conditions of the grant are being met and if the goal of the grant is likely to be achieved.

Grantee:

The individual or organization that receives a grant.

Grantor:

The individual or organization that makes a grant.

Grassroots Fundraising:

Efforts to raise money from individuals or groups from the local community on a broad basis. Usually an organization does grassroots fundraising within its own constituency—people who live in the neighborhood served or clients of the agency's services. Grassroots fundraising activities include membership drives, raffles, bake sales, auctions, dances and a range of other activities. Foundation managers often feel that successful grassroots fundraising indicates that an organization has substantial community support.

Guidelines:

A statement of a foundation's goals, priorities, criteria and procedures for applying for a grant.

In-Kind Contribution:

A donation of goods or services rather than cash or appreciated property.

Independent Foundation:

These private foundations are usually founded by one individual, often by bequest. They are occasionally termed "nonoperating" because they do not run their own programs. Sometimes individuals or groups of people, such as family members, form a foundation while the donors are still living. Many large independent foundations, such as the Ford Foundation, are no longer governed by members of the original donor's family but are run by boards made up of community, business and academic leaders.

Private foundations make grants to other tax-exempt organizations to carry out their charitable purposes. Private foundations must make charitable expenditures of approximately 5 percent of the market value of their assets each year. Although exempt from federal income tax, private foundations must pay a yearly excise tax of 1 or 2 percent of their net investment income. The Rockefeller Foundation and the John D. and Catherine T. MacArthur Foundation are two examples of well-known "independent" private foundations.

Intermediate Sanctions:

Penalty taxes applied to disqualified persons of public charities (see **Disqualified Person**) that receive an excessive benefit from financial transactions with the charity. An excessive benefit may result from overcompensation for services or from other transactions such as charging excessive rent on property rented to the charity. Unlike private foundations, public charities are not barred from engaging in financial transactions with disqualified persons as long as the transaction is fair to the charity. Penalty taxes also may apply to organization managers, such as the charity's board, that knowingly approve an excess benefit transaction.

Internal Revenue Service (IRS):

The federal agency with responsibility for regulating foundations and their activities.
On-line at **www.irs.gov**.

Jeopardy Investment:

An investment that risks the foundation's ability to carry out its exempt purposes. Although certain types of investments are subject to careful examination, no single type is automatically a jeopardy investment. Generally, a jeopardy investment is found to be made when a foundation's managers have failed to exercise ordinary business care and prudence. The result of a jeopardy investment may be penalty taxes imposed upon a foundation and its managers. (See **Program Related Investment**.)

Letter of Intent:

A grantor's letter or brief statement indicating intention to make a specific gift.

Leverage:

A method of grantmaking practiced by some foundations. Leverage occurs when a small amount of money is given with the express purpose of attracting funding from other sources or of providing the organization with the tools it needs to raise other kinds of funds. Sometimes known as the "multiplier effect."

Limited-Purpose Foundation:

A type of foundation that restricts its giving to one or very few areas of interest, such as higher education or medical care.

Loaned Executives:

Corporate executives who work for nonprofit organizations for a limited period of time while continuing to be paid by their permanent employers.

Lobbying:

Efforts to influence legislation by influencing the opinion of legislators, legislative staff and government administrators directly involved in drafting legislative proposals. The Internal Revenue Code sets limits on lobbying by organizations that are exempt from tax under Section 501(c)(3). Public charities (see **Public Charity**) may lobby as long as lobbying does not become a substantial part of their activities. Private foundations (see **Private Foundations**) generally may not lobby except in limited circumstances such as on issues affecting their tax-exempt status or the deductibility of gifts to them. Conducting nonpartisan analysis and research and disseminating the results to the public generally is not lobbying for purposes of these restrictions.

Matching Gifts Program:

A grant or contributions program that will match employees' or directors' gifts made to qualifying educational, arts and cultural, health or other organizations. Specific guidelines are established by each employer or foundation. (Some foundations also use this program for their trustees.)

Matching Grant:

A grant or gift made with the specification that the amount donated must be matched on a one-for-one basis or according to some other prescribed formula.

Operating Foundation:

Also called private operating foundations, operating foundations are private foundations that use the bulk of their income to provide charitable services or to run charitable programs of their own. They make few, if any, grants to outside organizations. To qualify as an operating foundation, specific rules, in addition to the applicable rules for private foundations, must be followed. The Carnegie Endowment for International Peace and the Getty Trust are examples of operating foundations.

Operating Support:

A contribution given to cover an organization's day-to-day, ongoing expenses, such as salaries, utilities, office supplies, etc.

Payout Requirement:

The minimum amount that a private foundation is required to expend for charitable purposes (includes grants and necessary and reasonable administrative expenses).
In general, a private foundation must pay out annually approximately 5 percent of the average market value of its assets.

Philanthropy:

Philanthropy is defined in different ways. The origin of the word philanthropy is Greek and means love for mankind. Today, philanthropy includes the concept of voluntary giving by an individual or group to promote the common good. Philanthropy also commonly refers to grants of money given by foundations to nonprofit organizations. Philanthropy addresses the contribution of an individual or group to other organizations that in turn work for the causes of poverty or social problems—improving the quality of life for all citizens. Philanthropic giving supports a variety of activities, including research, health, education, arts and culture, as well as alleviating poverty.

Pledge:

A promise to make future contributions to an organization. For example, some donors make multiyear pledges promising to grant a specific amount of money each year.

Post-Grant Evaluation:

A review of the results of a grant, with the emphasis upon whether or not the grant achieved its desired objective.

Preliminary Proposal:

A brief draft of a grant proposal used to learn if there is sufficient interest to warrant submitting a proposal.

Private Foundation:

A nongovernmental, nonprofit organization with funds (usually from a single source, such as an individual, family or corporation) and program managed by its own trustees or directors, established to maintain or aid social, educational, religious or other charitable activities serving the common welfare, primarily through grantmaking. U.S. private foundations are tax-exempt under Section 501(c)(3) of the Internal Revenue Code and are classified by the IRS as a private foundation as defined in the code.

Program Officer:

Also referred to as a corporate affairs officer, program associate, public affairs officer or community affairs officer, a program officer is a staff member of a foundation or corporate giving program who may do some or all of the following: recommend policy, review grant requests, manage the budget and process applications for the board of directors or contributions committee.

Program-Related Investment:

A loan or other investment made by a private foundation to a profitmaking or nonprofit organization for a project related to the foundation's stated purpose and interests. Program related investments are an exception to the general rule barring jeopardy investments. Often, program-related investments are made from a revolving fund; the foundation generally expects to receive its money back with limited, or below-market, interest, which then will provide additional funds for loans to other organizations. A program-related investment may involve loan guarantees, purchases of stock or other kinds of financial support.

Public Charity:

A nonprofit organization that is exempt from federal income tax under Section 501(c)(3) of the Internal Revenue Code and that receives its financial support from a broad segment of the general public. Religious, educational and medical institutions are deemed to be public charities. Other organizations exempt under Section 501(c)(3) must pass a public support test (see **Public Support Test**) to be considered public charities, or must be formed to benefit an organization that is a public charity (see **Supporting Organizations**). Charitable organizations that are not public charities are private foundations and are subject to more stringent regulatory and reporting requirements (see **Private Foundations**).

Public Foundation:

Public foundations, along with community foundations, are recognized as public charities by the IRS. Although they may provide direct charitable services to the public as other nonprofits do, their primary focus is on grantmaking. To be eligible for membership in the Council, a public foundation must grant at least $60,000 yearly and must dedicate at least 50 percent of its organizational budget to a competitive grantmaking program.

Public Support Test:

There are two public support tests, both of which are designed to ensure that a charitable organization is responsive to the general public rather than a limited number of persons. One test, sometimes referred to as 509(a)(1) or 170(b)(1)(A)(vi) for the sections of the Internal Revenue Code where it is found, is for charities like community foundations that mainly rely on gifts, grant, and contributions. To be automatically classed as a public charity under this test, organizations must show that they normally receive at least one-third of their support from the general public (including government agencies and foundations). However, an organization that fails the automatic test still may qualify as a public charity if its public support equals at least 10 percent of all support and it also has a variety of other characteristics—such as a broad-based board—that make it sufficiently "public." The second test, sometimes referred to as the section 509(a)(2) test, applies to charities, such as symphony orchestras or theater groups, that get a substantial part of their income from the sale of services that further their mission, such as the sale of tickets to performances. These charities must pass a one-third/one-third test. That is, they must demonstrate that their sales and contributions normally add up to at least one third of their financial support, but their income from investments and unrelated business activities does not exceed one-third of support.

Query Letter:

Also referred to as a letter of inquiry, this is a brief letter outlining an organization's activities and a request for funding sent to a prospective donor to determine if there is sufficient interest to warrant submitting a full proposal. This saves the time of the prospective donor and the time and resources of the prospective applicant. (See **Preliminary Proposal**.)

Restricted Funds:

Assets or income that is restricted in its use, in the types of organizations that may receive grants from it or in the procedures used to make grants from such funds.

Seed Money:

A grant or contribution used to start a new project or organization.

Self-Dealing:

A private foundation is generally prohibited from entering into any financial transaction with disqualified persons (see **Disqualified Person**). The few exceptions to this rule include paying reasonable compensation to a disqualified person for services that are necessary to fulfilling the foundation's charitable purposes. Violations will result in an initial penalty tax equal to 5 percent of the amount involved, payable by the self-dealer.

Site Visit:

Visiting a donee organization at its office location or area of operation and/or meeting with its staff or directors or with recipients of its services.

Social Investing:

Also referred to as ethical investing and socially responsible investing, this is the practice of aligning a foundation's investment policies with its mission. This may include making program-related investments and refraining from investing in corporations with products or policies inconsistent with the foundation's values.

Supporting Organization:

A supporting organization is a charity that is not required to meet the public support test because it supports a public charity. To be a supporting organization, a charity must meet one of three complex legal tests that assure, at a minimum, that the organization being supported has some influence over the actions of the supporting organization. Although a supporting organization may be formed to benefit any type of public charity, the use of this form is particularly common in connection with community foundations. Supporting organizations are distinguishable from donor-advised funds because they are distinct legal entities.

Tax-Exempt Organizations:

Organizations that do not have to pay state and/or federal income taxes. Organizations other than churches seeking recognition of their status as exempt under Section 501(c)(3) of the Internal Revenue Code must apply to the Internal Revenue Service. Charities may also be exempt from state income, sales and local property tax.

Technical Assistance:

Operational or management assistance given to a nonprofit organization. It can include fundraising assistance, budgeting and financial planning, program planning, legal advice, marketing and other aids to management. Assistance may be offered directly by a foundation or corporate staff member or in the form of a grant to pay for the services of an outside consultant. (See **In-Kind Contribution**.)

Tipping:

The situation that occurs when a gift or grant is made that is large enough to significantly alter the grantee's funding base and cause it to fail the public support test. Such a gift or grant results in "tipping" or conversion from public charity to private foundation status.

Trust:

A legal device used to set aside money or property of one person for the benefit of one or more persons or organizations.

Trustee:

The person(s) or institutions responsible for the administration of a trust.

Unrestricted Funds:

Normally found at community foundations, an unrestricted fund is one that is not specifically designated to particular uses by the donor, or for which restrictions have expired or been removed.

Compiled by *John Dickason* (MARKEY CHARITABLE TRUST AND CAMBRIDGE ASSOCIATES), consultants from a *Lexicon for Community Foundations* (COUNCIL ON FOUNDATIONS), *Glossary of Definitions and Terms* (CAMBRIDGE ASSOCIATES), *Finance and Investment Handbook* (BARRON'S) and other appropriate sources.

Index

A

Accountability, grantmakers	75
Actual need of grantseekers, determining	30-31
Advantages of grantmaking	10-11
Advice	
getting	10, 26
giving	7, 31, 41-42
gratuitous	7
Advisors, outside	24-25
Affinity groups and grantmaker associations	2, 82-83
Applicants. *See* Grantseekers	
Applications. *See* Proposals	
Approving grants. *See also* Board review and approval	25
Arrogance	7-8, 39
Audit reports	49, 54-56
Authority and power	
problems surrounding power	7
scope of	8, 43
Award letters	73

B

"Bad" recommendations	71-72
Behavior, unprofessional	7-8, 39
Benchmarking performance	78
Board meetings	
discussing the docket	71
self-evaluation following	76, 101
Board members. *See* Grantmaker board members; Grantseeker board members	
Board review and approval	
docket materials	70-71
failing to get approval	71-72
process	68-69

117

time frame and schedule	71
Budget, project	49, 51-54

C

Challenges to grantmakers	79
Communicating with grantseekers	8, 25
Communication skills	4, 71
Complex systems, unintended consequences in	10
Confidentiality	
obligations	72-73
of site visits	32
Consultants	
in self-evaluation	77
Corporate giving programs	
about	1-2
grantmaker portfolios	67-68
program guidelines	11-13
Cost-effectiveness of project	65
Council on Foundations	81
affinity groups and grantmaker associations	82-83
Credibility of proposals	20

D

Decisionmaking process, final. *See also*	
Board review and approval	8, 43
Decisionmaking skills	10
Denying grant requests/proposals	8, 17-19, 25
Docket materials	70-71
Due diligence	33

E

Ethics	79
Evaluating proposals. *See* Reviewing proposals	
Exemplary proposals	22
Expectations of others	8
Experts, use in reviewing proposals	24-25

F

Feasibility of proposals	20
Federal Form 990	49, 58-63
Final decisionmaking process. *See* also	
Board review and approval	8, 43

Financial analysis	
about	45
cost-effectiveness of project	65
and goals for financial reporting	46-47
making inquiries	46-47
math requirements	45-46
oddities of nonprofit finance	46
Financial discussions	47-48, 50, 64, 65
Financial reports	
about	49-50
audit reports	49, 54-56
Federal Form 990	49, 58-63
goals for reporting	46-47
organization-wide budget	49, 54
project budget	49, 51-54
recent financial statements	49, 56-57
Schedule A to Form 990	49
Financial statements	49, 56-57
Foundations	
about	1-2
grantmaker portfolios	67-68
program guidelines	11-13
Funding priorities	3-4
Funding strategy	3-4

G

Getting advice	10, 26
Giving advice	7, 31, 41-42
Glossary	103-115
Goal setting	78-79
Governance of grantseekers, quick reference guide	88
Grant agreements. *See also* Reporting requirements for grantees	73, 96-97
Grant applications. *See* Proposals	
Grant evaluation procedures	73-74
Grant recommendation summary	
about	67
accompanying docket materials	70-71
"bad" recommendations	71-72
contents	70
grantmaker effectiveness and	67
making mistakes	72

118 GRANTMAKING BASICS: A FIELD GUIDE FOR FUNDERS

risky grants	72-73
template	95

Grant requests. *See* Proposals

Grantees

meeting with existing	13
reporting requirements	73-74, 98-99
Grantmaker associations	82-83, 84

Grantmaker board members

funding priorities	3-4
relationship with	2-3, 25, 69
Grantmaker portfolios	67-68

Grantmakers. *See also* Professional development; Self-evaluation

about	1-2
accountability	75
challenges to	79
effectiveness	67
ethics	79
growing into the job	13-14
investing in the common good	67
learning from grantee reports	74
making mistakes	72
potential problems for	6-10
program guidelines and	11-13
role in final decisionmaking process	8, 43
skills and attributes	2-5
special opportunities for	10-11
workload	9-10
Grantmaking opportunities, external environment and	68
Grantmaking strategies	3-4, 13
Grantmaking trends	6
Grants, risky	72-73
Grantseeker board members, visits with	37, 64
Grantseeker financial officers, visits with	37, 64

Grantseekers

capability of	20
communication with	8, 25
determining actual need of	30-31
governance of	88
interview quick reference guide	87-90
learning about	29-30
meeting the people	28-29
persistent	19
personal relationship with	25
planning strategies of	87
staff capabilities and morale of	89-90
Gratuitous advice	7

I

Importance of proposed projects	20
Inappropriate proposals	17-19
Independent Auditor's Report sample	54-56
Information synthesis skills	4

Interviews. *See also* Site visits

quick reference guide	87-90
styles to avoid	39
Investing in the common good	67
Isolation	9

L

Leverage	11

Liabilities. *See* Potential problems

M

Math requirements, in financial analysis	45-46

Mistakes

in recommendations	72
in reviewing proposals	23
Money, relationships and	6-7

N

Nonprofit finance, oddities of	46

O

Occupational hazards	6-10
Oddities of nonprofit finance	46
Organization-wide budget	49, 54
Outside sources for reviewing proposals	24-25

P

Peers, consulting with	79

Performance measurement. *See* Self-evaluation

Persistent grantseekers	19
Personal relationship with grantseekers	25
Personality traits	4

Philanthropy
    about 5
    due diligence in 33
    unintended consequences of 10
Planning strategies of grantseekers,
    quick reference guide 87
Potential problems 6–10
Power. See Authority and power
Presentation skills 71
Professional development. See also Self-evaluation
Professional relationships 5–6, 30, 78–79
    consulting with peers 79
    developing 5–6
    outside reviewers and advisors 24–25
Program areas, familiarity with 3, 5, 30–32
Program guidelines 11–13
    expectations of others and 8
Program officers. See Grantmakers
Progress reports 73–74
Project budget. See Budget, project
Project cost-effectiveness 65
Projects, importance of proposed 20
Promise of funding, retracting 25
Proposal review worksheet. See also
    Reviewing proposals 85–86
Proposal-reviewing skills, improving 26
Proposals. See also Denying grant requests/proposals; Reviewing proposals
    categories of 20–21
    common problems 21–22
    credibility of 20
    exemplary 22
    feasibility of 20
    financial reports submitted with 49–63
    format 16
    purpose and function 15
    signal virtues of 20
Public declaration of program guidelines ... 11, 13

R

RAGs. See Regional associations of grantmakers
Regional associations of grantmakers (RAGs) 2, 25, 84
Relationships
    elements of 34
    with grantmaker board members 2–3, 25, 69
    money and 6–7
    personal relationship with grantseekers 25
    professional 5–6, 24–25, 79
Reporting requirements for grantees 73–74
    sample letter 98
    sample reporting guidelines 99
Research and self-directed study 5
Retracting a promise of funding 25
Reviewers and advisors, outside 24–25
Reviewing proposals. See also Board review and approval
    improving reviewing skills 26
    mistakes in reading 23
    overall process 19–21
    preliminary scanning 17, 19
    questions to ask while reading 20–21, 31
    reading for content 17, 31
    scrutinizing the proposal 19–20, 22–24
    using outside reviewers and advisors .. 24–25
Risky grants 72–73

S

Self-directed study and research 5
Self-evaluation
    benchmarking and 78
    following board meetings 76, 101
    methods for reviewing effectiveness ... 76–77
    panel of advisors for 77
    routine evaluation 75–76
    using outside evaluators/consultants ... 77
Self-improvement strategy 78–79
Self-motivation 5
Site visit arrangements 32
Site visit debriefing 43–44
Site visit goals 35
Site visit meetings
    with difficult people 37
    environment 34–35
    with grantseeker board members 37, 64
    managing the meetings 35–36
Site visit questions
    avoiding evasions 40

encountering untruths 40
making inquiries 38-39
pursuing unanswered questions 40
Site visit worksheet 91-94
Site visits
behavior to avoid 39
benefits of 28-31
confidentiality and 32
considerations 27-28
focusing on results 42
giving advice during 41-42
issues to explore 37-39
justified 27-28
maintaining focus during 35-36
making commitments during 43
observations to make 36, 40-41
preparing for 31-32
sample agenda 35
self-evaluation following 44
setting limits 32, 35, 40
staging 33-34
summary and departure 43
time limits 35
unjustified 28
unsuccessful 36
when to conclude 42
Skepticism in grantmaking 4
Skills and attributes of grantmakers 2-5
Special opportunities for grantmakers 10-11
Staff capabilities and morale of grantseekers,
quick reference guide 89-90

T

Time management skills 9-10
Timing and scheduling
for board review and approval 71
time allowance for reviews 8, 17
Trends in grantmaking 6
Turning down proposals. *See* Denying grant requests/proposals

U

Unexpected outcomes 74
Unintended consequences 10
Unprofessional behavior 7-8, 39
Urgent requests for proposal review 17

W

Workload 9-10